Harriet E. Francis

By Land and Sea

Incidents of Travel

Harriet E. Francis

By Land and Sea
Incidents of Travel

ISBN/EAN: 9783337210076

Printed in Europe, USA, Canada, Australia, Japan

Cover: Foto ©Andreas Hilbeck / pixelio.de

More available books at **www.hansebooks.com**

BY LAND AND SEA

INCIDENTS OF TRAVEL WITH CHATS ABOUT

HISTORY AND LEGENDS

BY

HARRIET

TROY N. Y.
NIMS AND KNIGHT
1891

AFFECTIONATELY INSCRIBED

TO THE GRANDCHILDREN

OF THE AUTHOR.

PREFACE.

The materials for this volume were gathered by MRS. JOHN M. FRANCIS of Troy, New York, during her residence abroad, while her husband was United States Minister at the Courts of Greece, Portugal and Austria-Hungary, and in a tour taken with him around the world. Unhappily, she did not live to superintend the publication of this work. But those who are aware of the purpose she had in view in preparing it are permitted to state that whatever of novelty or freshness there may be in her presentation of facts is the result of personal observation.

Quick to apprehend the characteristic traits of a people or a country, she might easily have expanded these pages with an array of details and statistics. But this was not her object. She desired primarily to enlarge the scope of the youthful mind by leading it to look away from itself and its environments to a study of this spacious world of ours. The first element in such a process is to interest. It was, therefore, not a geography, a gazetteer, nor a formal work of travel that she proposed, but a simple sketch of the chief points which attracted her in some of the countries she visited, so expressed as to fix the attention of the young, and, by first diverting them, to end by instructing and leading them to develop an interest in the history, topography and peoples of all parts of the world. Or, in other words, to quote from her own incompleted preface :

"It is proposed by the author to have some chats with the young people on various subjects relating to history and the natural physical wonders of the world, introducing incidents of travel and several interesting tales translated from foreign languages. The chats will be arranged in chapters--hoping by this system of short readings not to weary the young reader."

The fragmentary letters were compiled from correspondence with her children, relating to scenes and incidents coming under her observation during her sojourn abroad. There is no attempt at elaborate description, only salient points receiving attention, the object of the letters being to furnish in a familiar, conversational manner information most likely to interest or amuse the reader.

With this statement of its purpose the volume is commended to the public, hoping it will meet with the results intended by the lamented author.

JOHN M. FRANCIS.

CONTENTS.

PAGE.

Chat I. Across the Atlantic to England, - - 1
" II. France, Spain, and Portugal, - - - 9
" III. Switzerland, Austria, and Norway, - 24
" IV. Greece, - - - - - - - - - - 40
" V. Turkey, - - - - - - - - 51
" VI. Egypt, - - - - - - - - - - 61
" VII. Arabia and India, - - - - 79
" VIII. China, - - - - - - - - - - 99
" IX. Japan, - - - - - - - - 115
" X. Home once More, - - - - - - 126

FRAGMENTARY LETTERS.

Utah, - - - - - - 139
California, - - - - - - 141
Japan, - - - - - - 146
China, - - - - - - - 152
Singapore, - - - - - - 161
Ceylon, - - - - - - - 164
Egypt, - - - - - - 167
Austria, - - - - - - - 175
Hungary, - - - - - - 180
Bohemia, - - - - - - - 184
Portugal, - - - - - - 191

ILLUSTRATIONS.

PAGE.

1. Lisbon, Portugal, - - - - - - - - 18
2. Chamouni, Switzerland, - - - - - - 24
3. The Acropolis, Athens, - - - - - - 40
4. Mars Hill, Athens, - - - - - - - 44
5. The Golden Horn from Pera, - - - - 52
6. Snake Charmers in Benares, India, - - - 80
7. An Indian carriage and pair, Bombay, - 82
8. The Burning Ghat on the Ganges at Benares, 84
9. A Hindoo mother and children—Group of Indian men and women in Bombay, India, - - 86
10. Banyan Tree at Barrackpore, near Calcutta, India, - - - - - - - - - - 88
11. State Elephants of the Viceroy equipped for a Journey, Benares, - - - - - - 90
12. The Taj at Agra, India, - - - - - - 92
13. A Corridor in the Palace at Agra, India, - 94
14. The Kutub Minar—A Corridor of the Mosque near the Kutub Minar, Delhi, India, - 96
15. The Audience Chamber in the Palace at Agra, 98
16. Japanese Bed-room Scenes, - - - - - 118
17. A Jinrikshaw and Chinese Barber, - - 122
18. Niagara Falls, - - - - - - - - 130
19. The Great Japanese Idol of Diabutsa at Kamakura, near Yokohama, - - - - - 150
20. A Chinese Junk, - - - - - - - - 154
21. Natives of Singapore, - - - - - - 160
22. The Entrance to the Whampoo Gardens, Singapore, 162
23. Jewel Peddlers at Point-de-Galla, Island of Ceylon, - - - - - - - - - - - 164
24. The Exterior of the Pavilion of the Palace at Gezeereh, Cairo, - - - - - - 170
25. The Pyramid of Cheops, the Sphynx and Temple of Chafra, Cairo, - - - - - - 172
26. Entrance of the Monserrate Palace and the Square of D. Pedro, Lisbon, - - - 192

BY LAND AND SEA.

CHAT I

ACROSS THE ATLANTIC TO ENGLAND.

AMONG THE ROLLING BILLOWS—AT THE MERSEY'S MOUTH—VAST LONDON—A CITY THAT FIVE MILLIONS OF PEOPLE CALL HOME—THE ABBEY AND THE CATHEDRAL—THE GREAT WHITE TOWER—THROUGH ENGLISH PARKS TO SHAKESPEARE'S HOME—AN INN WHOSE EVERY ROOM IS A DRAMA—WHERE AN IMMORTAL POET LIVED AND LOVED—A QUEEN'S HUGE CASTLE-HOME—SPLENDOR IN CHINA, PORCELAIN AND GOLD—THE CAPITAL OF FRANCE AND THE TOMB OF NAPOLEON—WEDDING-PARTIES AMONG THE TREES—TURNING SOUTHWARD.

Let us begin our chat by sailing for England, following the path by which I first visited the Old World.

About noontime I went on board the great four-masted steamship that was soon to cast off from the dock and move slowly away from her moorings. The Stars and Stripes were floating proudly from the masthead; scores of loving hands were waving the last good-by, signal answering signal, and even some of the sturdy old tars were seen to wipe away unbidden tears as they took a farewell look at their wives and little ones who have come down to the wharf to see the ship off. The baggage is hurried on the deck, and tons of mail bags are tossed after the boxes and trunks. The passengers go below to open the steamer trunks, and arrange for the necessities of the voyage, before it becomes too rough to attend to these little duties.

As we approach Sandy Hook dinner is announced; the seats at table are all occupied. Some of the inexperienced sea-travelers remark on the insufficient table service. Overhearing this, an old voyager says: "It will be all right in a day or two, my friends. To-morrow there will be more waiters than diners." "How can that be?" ventured to ask a fair young girl who is making her first sea voyage. "Old Neptune will find us out by to-morrow, and in all probability will escort us a part of the way over. And when the old sea-dog comes out, many of the ladies remain in their cabins," said the traveler. When we crossed the foaming bar and passed out on the broad ocean I counted a score or more of ships, large and small, ploughing through the briny deep in all directions; some freighted to overflowing with human beings, and others loaded to the water's edge with rich products from the far-off Indies on their way to America.

But soon our stately steamship began to toss and dip her prow deep in the sea, rise up and ride majestically over the mountain waves as they rolled higher and higher, now and then throwing a tremendous sea on the deck. However, I felt but little anxiety, confident of the strength of the great ship, and of the skill of the navigators of our time, who know well how to overcome the dangers of the sea.

In less than a week, so swiftly do these splendid steamships now cross the Atlantic, we saw the green fields of "Merry old England" as we sailed up the channel and arrived at the entrance of the port of Liverpool, which lies at the mouth of the river Mersey. We took a pilot who safely guided the vessel to her dock, and in an hour we were on shore, bag and baggage, and hurried to the railway station. There we took a train for

London, anxious for a peep at the greatest city in the world, although we would gladly have waited a few hours to see more of Liverpool, and visit the quaint old city of Chester, which is not far distant.

We arrived in London after dark. As we rode rapidly in a carriage from street to street until we reached our hotel, I was overwhelmed with the vastness of this wonderful capital and the endless crowds which thronged its labyrinth of streets. There are many entire countries, any one of which does not contain as many people as the city of London. Its population is about five millions.

One of the most important sights of London is the Astronomical Observatory at Greenwich, on the river Thames. It is one of the landmarks of the earth, for time and distance are reckoned from this observatory, calculations of which are accepted by more than half the world.

Following the Thames I took a glance at Westminster Abbey, one of the most renowned buildings in England. The Abbey is of the Gothic style of architecture, and is more than one hundred years older than St. Paul's Cathedral. It was built in the early part of 1500. Its walls enclose the sepulchre of the royal family and the tombs and monuments of many of England's most celebrated poets and statesmen.

The dome of St. Paul's Cathedral is easily distinguished by its size and height from other massive buildings in London. It is next in size to St. Peter's at Rome. St. Paul's is five hundred feet and St. Peter's six hundred and thirty feet long. The height from the ground to the extreme top of St. Paul's is three hundred and sixty-five feet ; St. Peter's lifts its cross four hundred and thirty-seven feet from its base. When Sir Christopher Wren was excavating for the foundation walls of St. Paul's Cathedral in 1675, he found relics of an older structure.

It is not yet determined exactly when the earlier church was built.

Another edifice of great interest is the Tower of London, sometimes called the White Tower because of its color. It is said to have had its origin at the time when Julius Cæsar invaded England, although it has been much changed since then. The servitors and custodians wear richly-colored clothes of the style worn in the time of Queen Elizabeth. The crown jewels, including the famous Koh-i-noor diamond, are kept there and shown to visitors; in another gallery is a row of mounted figures in the mail armor of the days of chivalry. But to one who reads English history the chief interest of this ancient structure is in the fact that it was for centuries the place where prisoners of state were confined, and executed when condemned. Anne Boleyn, Sir Thomas More, Sir Walter Raleigh and many other characters famous in history pined and suffered within these grim old walls.

Among various excursions which we made when in England was a visit to the renowned birthplace of Shakespeare at Stratford-on-Avon. It is a journey of three hours by rail from London. There were extensive parks, clumps of venerable oaks and elms, picturesque old water mills, quaint old villages with their gray stone churches, little old thatch-roofed cottages with moss-covered walls, and many other features of English scenery appearing before us as we passed through the country.

We took lodgings in the Shakespeare Inn, the identical tavern where the poet went daily for his cup of sack. Time has made its ravages in the old building. There have been some additions to it, but in the general character of the rooms we were told no change had been made. All the rooms are named from the poet's plays, each having its name printed in black letters over the door. My room was the "Romeo and Juliet" chamber; a friend who was with us was lodged in

'All's Well that Ends Well;" another friend occupied the "King Lear" chamber. The coffee-room is called "As You Like It;" the family sitting-room is named the "Merry Wives of Windsor;" the tap-room has over the door "Measure for Measure." One bed-room is named the "Desdemona" chamber, and so on, until the forty rooms of the house are all designated.

If we believe what is told us, the old house is still conducted as it was in the great poet's time. The bedrooms remain unchanged in size, and, judging from the appearance of the furniture in the rooms I occupied, there has been but little change in it. I am sure the modern toilet of a lady could not be made in one of these small bedrooms. The window-panes are five by six inches, and are set in very heavy sashes. Everything in and about the house indicates antiquity.

We visited the house in which the immortal poet was born. The old servant there informed us that it "looks just as it did when the baby William lay there in his cradle." The house is now used as a museum for Shakespeare's relics. We went to the church where the poet was baptized. On one of the pews is a metal plate on which is engraved the name of the poet's father. We also visited Shottery, the little farm-house where Anne Hathaway's parents lived, about a mile from the village. The young poet, little suspecting his future renown, made frequent excursions thither to pay court to Mistress Anne, whom he afterwards married and who was his senior by several years. A descendent of the Hathaway family--an old lady far along in her seventies—occupied the old house when we visited it. She called our attention to the well, the very same out of which the family drew water in olden times. She showed us a few pieces of old delft ware which was used by the family in the days when William was accustomed to sup there. In reply to the question if one or two of those articles could be bought, the good old lady said, "Not for any money." We sat upon the same settee in the chimney-corner on which the young poet and Mistress Anne sat many a time. I can accept the age of the old bench, for it has been strengthened on all sides with bands of iron, and the back legs are kept in place by two thick hickory blocks.

Not far from Stratford is Warwick Castle, one of the finest remains of the feudal times to be seen in Europe. It is famous as the stronghold of the great Duke of Warwick, known as the King-maker, on account of his power in the long and terrible wars of the Roses. On our return to London we visited another famous castle, now a royal palace. It is at Windsor, an hour's ride by rail from London, and Queen Victoria resides there most of the time. We were shown the State apartments, the Queen's drawing and dining rooms, and the chambers just made ready for the Princess Beatrice and Prince Henry of Battenberg. The latter suite of rooms is called the "bridal apartment" and it is always given to the last married couple of the royal family. Nothing more cosy and comfortable can be imagined than this beautiful apartment. The sitting-room is elegant and cheerful in crimson velvet and gold decorations. The lovely little morning-room is prettily furnished in pink and white satin. The stately bed-chamber is upholstered in blue satin, with silver cord and tassel trimmings. The baths are marble. From the windows are seen vistas of stately old elms, and wide stretches of green lawns, with here and there beds of flowers. Beyond, one sees the noble forests of Windsor Park, with countless sheep grazing quietly on its lawns.

The castle is very extensive. The building covers twenty-two acres, and is perhaps the largest in Europe. When the Queen is at Windsor, four hundred servants, including three head cooks, are employed there. Each chief cook has his own kitchen and assistants. One of the finest collections in the world of the famous Sevres ware and antique porcelains is to be seen at Windsor castle. It is arranged in large ebony cabinets, lined with cream-colored satin. There are no less than forty-five of these cabinets in the different drawing-rooms and in the portrait gallery; the Queen's drawing-rooms, four in all, have cabinets of choice porcelain along the four sides of the walls. We were shown the china pantry. This is a large room with shelves from floor to ceiling, filled with rich and costly old and new china. Of the porcelain in use there are ten services of rich Sevres, each of which is sufficient for a banquet of one hundred and fifty guests. This is splendid indeed.

In the banqueting hall, adjoining the Queen's apartments, is a punch bowl made of thirteen thousand ounces of pure silver, and heavily plated inside and outside with gold.

Now let us visit Paris. It is a wonderful city to look upon, with its magnificent buildings, lovely avenues and gardens, its fine old cathedrals and numerous church spires. Beautiful Paris is the queen of cities. Among the many conspicuous edifices is the Hotel des Invalides, the resting place of the remains of Napoleon Bonaparte. In this mausoleum, at noon every day, a military burial salute is given by the Napoleon Guard in remembrance of the great French hero. When I witnessed this solemn ceremony, some years ago, there was still among the platoon of soldiers one tottering old man who had served under the famous general.

Paris is not the gay city that it was during the empire. The political situation is too unsettled to allow much attention to be given to its adornment, or even in preserving that which remains of the olden times. One of the most interesting buildings of the former Paris—the Tuilleries—exists no more as a palace. A portion of the building is now occupied as official bureaus. The gardens, however, are still well kept, although the absence of the once beautiful palace detracts much from their beauty.

The splendid boulevard called the Champs Elysees—leading up to the Arc de Triomphe—is always bright with throngs of gay equipages and animated with amusing street spectacles. The Bois de Boulogne is a lovely park. It covers a large area and some parts are preserved to appear like wild forest land. The Bois de Vincennes is still the favorite place for the bridal tour of wedding parties among a certain class of Parisian shop-people. The bride and groom with a few favorite attendants, immediately after the marriage, which occurs in the chapel near the park, take a walk through the beautiful groves. The wedding party with uncovered heads, the bride's veil wafting to and fro with the fancy of the winds, present a very romantic picture.

One might linger for months amused by the many interesting ancient and modern spectacles of the gay capital of France; but there is yet much for us to see in our wanderings, and we must proceed onward and southward.

CHAT II.

FRANCE—SPAIN—PORTUGAL.

The Vine-Covered Hills of Southern France—Castles and Bandit-Caves—Across the Spanish Border—A Robber-Band Surrounds a Diligence—How a Countess Saved Her Treasures—Money in an Englishman's Boots—A Dinner-Party with Jewels for Souvenirs—The Storied Alhambra—Spain's Centre—Madrid—Foot-Washing at Seville—Canvass that Master Painters made Beautiful—The Fame of Portuguese History—Cork and Tiles—How Ulysses Founded Lisbon—The Queen and the Diamond Counterfeiter—Driving Turkeys to Market—Pelted at the Carnival—Flour and Perfumed Water—Missiles from all Hands—Ladies Barefooted in a Religious Procession—Oporto—Students and their Caps—Fishwomen Adorned with Gold and Silver—Pilgrims Climbing on their Knees to the Shrine on the Mountain-Top.

Rushing over the railway past many a lovely valley, and many an old castle crumbling on picturesque heights, we at last reach the south of France and look upon one of the pleasantest parts of the European Continent, where some beautiful pictures are brought to view, linked with interesting remembrances.

The slopes of this long mountain range dividing France and Spain, and extending through some of Spain's richest possessions, are intensely picturesque. The pretty, vine-clad villas, the romantic old chateaus, the little villages of the mountains, walled in with laden fruit trees, the groves of chestnuts, the many miles of mulberry trees festooned with white and purple fruit, offer a pretty panoramic view to look upon. And now and then may be seen a little hamlet with its church spire towering high above the low cottages.

And again, far above the gardens of the Pyrenees, rise famous old castles with their turreted towers, many of them long since reduced to ruins, but still interesting to look upon. Interspersed among these old ruins are many grottos and caverns, which formerly were the dens of the bandits ; and perhaps even in our days may be found some of these human terrors. We don't like robber stories, and none should enter into our chats, but I must relate an incident that occurred not many years ago, for it is amusing rather than thrilling.

The story was told me by a French lady who witnessed the scene. This lady, Madame ——, was making a day's journey in a diligence over one of the mountain roads in the lower Pyreneean range. Among the half-dozen passengers was a Spanish countess and an Englishman. The countess was dressed in the garb of an humble peasant, and in her appearance gave no indication of her station in life.

The day had passed without incident or unusual adventure until just at night-fall, when suddenly a peculiar signal was sounded by the post—horn a signal that is given by the coachman when he discovers at a distance a band of suspicious looking men, and it is well understood by Spaniards. The disguised countess quickly remarked that if any of the passengers had money or jewels with them they should dispose of them as best they could, in order to save them from the bandits.

The Englishman said he had four thousand pounds in bank notes with him and asked how he should hide his money. The countess told him to take off his boots, pull out the inner soles and lay the bank notes in between the soles and put them on again. He did as recommended, even the countess assisting him so as to hasten the work.

In a few minutes the diligence had overtaken the men, and immediately four stalwart bandits, disguised, seized the horses by the bits, while others presented themselves at the doors of the carriage. They politely saluted the passengers, saying smilingly, "Your money or your lives, gentlemen." All denied having any money. The countess with an innocent look pointed to the Englishman's boots, giving a certain signal, and said, "Gentlemen, examine his boots." The bank notes were quickly found and taken, whereupon the bandits thanked the gentleman for having so much money with him, and quietly disappeared in the thicket, believing they had secured all the treasure in the diligence, and that the informer was one of their band.

As soon as the diligence had got under way again, the Englishman showed great indignation, as did the other passengers also, and all were loud in their expressions of anger that the informer had suggested to their fellow traveler where to conceal his money, and then without hesitation had disclosed the fact.

After this free and certainly not uncalled-for expression on the part of the occupants of the diligence, the countess told him who she was, corroborating her statement by showing a paper of identification. She said that she had taken this means to save herself from the robbers, as she had with her a much larger sum of money than the gentleman had lost, and that she would with pleasure restore the full amount, and regarded herself as very fortunate that she was able to save the larger part of her own treasure, all of which would certainly have been taken from her, as the bandits generally examined every unprotected person who came in their way on the high roads, adding that she had resorted to this ruse, not only to save a part of her own treasure but also as a protection to the other passengers by giving out the idea that she belonged to the bandits' band, and had procured the information as to who in the diligence had money.

After the explanation of what certainly appeared to be a gross act of treachery, the countess invited the company to dine with her on the following day in her chateau in the town where all were to leave the diligence, and would be obliged to remain a day awaiting the next post conveyance, at the same time remarking that not one of her traveling companions would finally regret the disagreeable adventure.

At the hour designed on the next day the invited guests presented themselves at the chateau, not knowing whether a snarl or a pleasure was in store for them. The countess received them in a splendid audience room, and at once presented the Englishman not only with his lost four thousand pounds, but an additional thousand, and to each of her guests a valuable jewel.

The dinner episode was charming, and the guests departed delighted.

Being on the frontier of Spain, let us take a glance at that country on our way to Portugal. We may think of Spain as being richer in historic lore and works of art than in the beauty of its landscapes. A large part of the Spanish domain is covered with olive, cork and chestnut groves. All of these products are, as we know, in demand the world over. The greatest treasures of Spain are its Alhambra and picture galleries.

The Alhambra, which is in the city of Granada, is mentioned in the early historic annals of Spain. It was the palace of the ancient Moorish Kings. There is a record of the existence of a part of the palace in 864, when it was spoken of as a "terrestrial paradise." To form an idea of what it must have been in the magnificence of its early days one must imagine himself in the palaces of "Arabian Nights" renown as pictured in these fairy tales.

But large additions have been made from time to time to this most interesting edifice. This monument of such interest and splendor has been immortalized by the magic pen of one of our own authors, Washington Irving.

Madrid is situated about the center of the dominion. A little church stands just outside the city, which occupies, it is said, the exact central point of Spain. The city rests on high ground, and the soil, for nearly a hundred miles in every direction, is sandy, rocky and arid, and cannot be cultivated to any extent.

Seville is a beautiful city. The ceremonies of the Roman church are celebrated here more fully and more strictly than in any other European city. The religious ceremony of foot-washing, according to the Bible tradition, is still observed here as well as in Austria. When we reach Vienna we may be able to witness this most remarkable ceremonial at more leisure than we can give to it in this evening's chat.

There is a beautiful drive in the heart of Madrid, called the Patiro, where magnificent turnouts may be seen and beautiful women wearing mantillas on their heads instead of bonnets. The Madrid picture gallery contains one of the finest collections in the world. Masterpieces by Murillo, Titian, Tintoretto, Velasquez, Raphael, Rembrandt, Rubens, Van Dyck, Teniers, Guido Reni and other renowned painters are there. How much one may learn by studying the works of those masters!

From Spain to Portugal is but a step, comparatively speaking. Portugal is a small country but has a brave people. The hidalgos, or nobility of olden times, were a heroic race. Heroism and bravery are emblazoned all over the national history. Spain had her Columbus and Ponce de Leon; Portugal had her

Vasco da Gama, and her national poet Camoens. The Portuguese were the first European navigators of the waters of the East Indies since the time of Alexander the Great. They made discoveries of islands and countries which had never seen the Christian cross until raised by the Portuguese pioneers.

The peninsula comprising Spain and Portugal has experienced frightful earthquakes at times. The earthquake at Lisbon of 1755 was one of the most terrible in its consequences of any known in the history of the world. It is said that more than 60,000 persons perished that day.

A large portion of Portugal is covered with cork and olive groves. The commerce in cork is one of its largest industries. The landscape everywhere is picturesque. The valleys are covered with grapes, and the highlands with olive and cork forests.

Many of the houses in the larger cities, and, also in the smaller towns, are faced outside with bright-colored tiles laid on in picturesque designs, often in Moorish and sometimes in floral patterns. The effect under the bright sunlight is brilliant, the colors glistening like precious stones. In some of the old palaces the inside walls are covered with blue and white tiling halfway up the ceiling, depicting battle scenes, pictures from family life and noted historic events.

I found in an old Portuguese book the following very interesting legend respecting the founding of the city of Lisbon :

It is related that Ulysses, the hero of Greek history, with a band of followers, during his long wanderings on the seas endeavoring to find his native isle, Ithaca, after the conquest of Troy, came into the River Tagus. Here he found the harbor so delightful, after his long and dangerous buffetings on the seas, and the products along the shores so satisfying to his half-famished men, that he determined to trace out and occupy a city close by the shore. This he did, and erected a temple to

Minerva, naming the new city Ulysippo. The intruding customs and the overbearing manners of the Greeks at last drew upon them the hostility of the natives, and Ulysses was compelled to abandon the hope of making a permanent settlement in this genial climate, and induced his men—many of whom were inclined to remain with the natives—to sail again in search of his beloved Island of Ithaca, always hoping once more to meet Penelope and Telemachus, his wife and son, from whom he had been separated so many years.

An interesting tale is related of one of the early queens of Portugal, which has been immortalized by Auber in the opera of "Crown Diamonds." The story is dated in the year 1700; the scene is laid in Portugal. The opera is in three acts. The first act is located in the Estremadura mountains; the second in the Castle of the Duke de Campo-Mayor, in Coimbra; and the third act in the royal palace in Lisbon.

The story goes as follows: The young queen of Portugal, still in her minority, becomes aware of the embarrassed circumstances of the Kingdom, and resolves upon a novel way to assist the pecuniary condition of her country. She hears of a man who has been sentenced to death for coining false money. She has him secretly brought before her and tells him she will spare him life if he will make an imitation of the crown jewels, but it is to be done under the strictest secrecy, and so perfectly that the deception shall not be discovered. Thereupon the condemned man collects his band of workmen, and chooses for his laboratory a deep cavern in the rocks of the Estremadura mountains beneath an old hermitage.

In the garb of a gypsy girl, the young princess from time to time visits the secluded cavern under the pretense of going to the chapel in the hermitage, and carries to the counterfeiter each time some of the diamonds of which he is to make the imitation.

In the meanwhile an accident occurs to one of the hidalgos or nobility, who chances to be traveling in that country and has been thrown from his carriage and seriously hurt. He is brought to the hermitage for rest. Accidentally he falls through a trap-door into the cave where the men are at work, and the gypsy princess happens to be there at the same time. The young nobleman is obliged to remain some time in the cavern before he can be removed ; he becomes enamored of the pretty gypsy girl, who does not repel his advances, for she knows full well who her companion is. However, the time comes for them to separate. The young man swears that he will not divulge what he has seen in the cavern, and the princess gives him one of the real jewels as a souvenir, and requests him never to part with it.

The false jewels are at last finished, and the chief of the band, with the disguised princess, starts for Lisbon. Meanwhile the crown jewels are missed, and the country is filled with armed police searching for the robbers. The chief and the gypsy are arrested on suspicion and taken to Coimbra, where they are brought before the Minister of Justice. There the nobleman meets the gypsy girl, for he, too, is under temporary arrest, it having been discovered that he is wearing on his finger one of the lost jewels. He is greatly surprised to see her with the chief of the band of supposed robbers, but through the influence of the nobleman, she and the counterfeiter obtained a reprieve.

All hurry on to Lisbon to sue for mercy before the queen, who has just been declared to have attained her majority and is soon to be crowned.

During this time the real jewels have been sent abroad for sale, and the false ones have been substituted in their place.

The young queen is crowned. On the day of her coronation the revelation of the plot occurs, when the queen most satisfactorily explains her plan for replenishing the royal treasury, and her course is approved. The young hidalgo appears before the queen to sue for pardon, and is surprised to discover that the queen and the gypsy girl are the same person ; and a second and greater surprise awaits him when the queen chooses him for her husband, and says : "All is well ; nothing is false but the jewels I wear, and this is for the good of the country."

One of the curious sights of Lisbon is the Turkey Market, which is held during the winter months. The turkeys are driven in numbers of a hundred "bills" or more through the streets by old women and barefooted children. They are counted and spoken of as "bills," just as we speak of so many head of cattle. At the well-known cry of the venders, "Who wants to buy a turkey?" cooks hurry to the streets to make selections, and ladies in carriages and on the promenade order the turkey-drivers to pass their houses and leave them so many "bills."

When I was in Lisbon the carnival occurred in February. It was a very entertaining sight, as I saw it from a balcony of the Chiado or Broadway of Lisbon. One of the absurd amusements was throwing flour at each other. Those engaged in that sport protected their heads with caps drawn tightly over them, and donned clothing that could be washed, while the furniture was removed into back rooms. But no one could avoid the play of the bisuagas or small syringes through which perfumed water was ejected. Children frequently salute their parents in the early morning during the carnival with a sprinkling from the bisuagas.

In the house opposite us were a dozen men and women covered with flour from head to foot. Long before six o'clock, the hour when the carnival was to terminate, those people were ghastly white, and moved about in clouds of flying flour. Small paper bags containing flour are often thrown upon the people passing in the streets, while others are hurled at those seated or standing at the windows of the opposite houses. Persons thus assailed have no other redress than to return the pelting. Everything is considered as fair play during the last day of the carnival.

Small bags of beans and corn are often tossed into the carriages as disguised acquaintances are discovered passing each other in the street. I saw a peck of beans showered upon the crowd beneath the balcony of the house across the street. Sacks of squares of colored paper, cut very fine by machinery, are often dropped upon the heads of the passers-by, making pretty effects as they flutter about. Another pretty spectacle consists of showers of silver and gilt-tinsel paper, in small pieces, dropped from the roofs of the houses and wafted about the Chiado in the bright sunlight by the breezes, and lighting here and there upon the merry crowd below, like so many falling gold and silver stars. Nosegays, with mottoes or *billets doux* hidden among the flowers, are also thrown at those who may be recognized through their disguise. Another cunning device for carnival sport, is small balls made of fine cut paper, saturated with perfumed water, and used as carnival missiles and hurled at each other; these balls explode as they strike, and the wet paper flies apart and sticks fast wherever it falls.

During the last three hours of the carnival everyone becomes wild with excitement, and consequently great liberty is allowed. Nobody takes offense at anything, knowing well that the only way to escape the inconveniences of carnival sports is to remain at home. Naturally, however, everybody wants to see the sport, and of course is assailed everywhere. Not only do the people of the lower classes participate in these sportive contentions, but ladies and gentlemen in the highest society disguise and mask themselves and join the wild throng in the Chiado. Often entire families give way to the carnival craze

LISBON, PORTUGAL.

and go along the streets hurling beans and corn at persons in carriages and on the balconies.

The grand finale of the carnival is deferred until evening, when the theaters become centers of festivities. San Carlos, the royal opera house, has its parquet floored over, and dancing begins there at nine o'clock to end at midnight. Sometimes the members of the royal family participate in the amusements of the evening from the royal box; and they, too, are subject to the play of the bisuaga, without showing any resentment, and pleasantly join in the general pelting of the people about them. Those attending these balls are masked and wear dominos, and everybody is armed with bisuagas.

During the last three days of the carnival I did not dare to venture out in an open carriage. Once when riding in a close coach the door was daringly opened and a bisuaga was fired at me. A little farther on the carriage door was again opened, and a coil of muddy string was thrown on my lap and quickly drawn out, leaving a dirty track on my dress.

It is a puzzle to foreigners to learn the names of many of the streets in Lisbon, for some of them are spoken of by a name entirely different from that displayed on the sign board. For instance, the street named *Rua Bella da Rainba*, or the Beautiful Street of the Queen, is generally called *Rua da Prata*, Silver Street. Some of the street names are also absurdly long and inconvenient, such as *Rua da Santo Antonia do Convento do Coracao de Jesus*, Street of St. Antonio on the Square of the Convent of the Heart of Jesus. There are also some names of odd meaning, such as the street of the Onions and street of the Happily Married. One may learn considerable of the Portuguese language by studying the street names.

The religious processions were formerly among the most striking sights of Lisbon. But the later laws of Portugal have resulted in decreasing the power of the Roman Catholic Church in that country and with it the number and splendor of its street processions. One of the chief processions nowadays is that of Corpus Christi. It represents our Savior on his way to the crucifixion. There are six different figures of Christ in wood, carried upon as many platforms, decorated with natural and artificial flowers. Each platform is borne by eight priests with uncovered heads, preceded by a little girl about eight years old, dressed to represent an angel; she wears a bright blue dress and shoes of the same color; two silver paper wings are attached to her shoulders and a wreath of white roses crowns her head.

The first figure of Christ was dressed in a long purple robe, representing him as a teacher. The second was in a kneeling position and had a green branch in its hand. The third figure had a long, heavy rope around its waist. The fourth was naked and the feet and hands were bound with ropes. The figure on the fifth platform was bent and bore a heavy cross. The last figure represented Christ nailed to the cross. Then followed the figure of Mary, the mother. Behind these figures walked several men and women doing penance They had made vows that if certain prayers were answered, they would go through the streets barefooted in the procession and afterward dispense with shoes for a certain length of time. Among the penitents was a lady of nobility wearing a long black veil over her head and face, and carrying a crucifix in her hand. I observed that her feet were white and very delicate, and evidently unaccustomed to the hard pavement. There was a large military escort, and thousands of peeple moved in the procession.

In the pleasant month of May we made an excursion to Oporto, going by rail. The distance between the two capitals, as Lisbon and Oporto are called, is one hundred and eighty miles, but it requires thirteen hours to accomplish the journey, owing to the slow running time and frequent stops. We saw thousands of men, women and children laboring in the vineyards and grain fields, the scenery being everywhere very beautiful. In the neighborhood of Oporto is the district where the famous port wine is produced, and we saw grapes cultivated on all sides.

We stopped at Coimbra on the way. It is a most interesting university town, picturesquely built on a hillside by the banks of the lovely river Mandego. Many hundred students attend the University of Coimbra. One meets them everywhere on the streets. They are very polite in manner and always ready to reply to inquiries. While at college, the students do not wear hats in summer or winter. The uniform is a plain black suit, comprising a long black frock-coat and a Spanish cap having long tabs, one of which can be thrown over the left shoulder and the other in bad weather over the head.

Oporto is built on the steep banks of the Douro river, three miles from the mouth, and presents a very handsome appearance. The houses are generally faced outside with *azulejos* or glazed tiles of bright colors and Moorish patterns. Every window has its balcony, and the eaves project so far that they really offer a protection from rain to the passers-by. The entrances to the houses are low and dark. One of the finest streets of Oporto is occupied almost entirely by the gold and silver trade. Beautiful filigree ornaments are made there out of those metals. The women fish-venders wear neck-chains, ear-rings, finger-rings and large brooches either of gold or silver, even going without hat and shoes, and scarce skirt enough to cover their knees. But with these ornaments and a gay scarf around the waist the brown-complexioned women look quite bonny.

In Oporto the carrying business is done by oxen driven by barefooted and bareheaded old women and little girls, who handle dexterously the long switches with which they hasten the steps of the slow-moving animals. From Oporto we drove in a diligence to Braza, an interesting old cathedral town. From Braza we rode in a horse-railroad car to the foot of a mountain, where we took a cable elevator car that conveyed us by a very steep ascent twelve hundred feet higher, to the celebrated shrine and resort of pilgrims called Bon Jesus, or the Good Jesus. We found comfortable lodging at the Hotel do Bon Jesus. But the beds were hard as straw beds can be. Spring beds and hair mattresses have not found their way into that part of Portugal. The pillows were little cushions about twelve inches square, one on a bed, about as thick as a biscuit, and the pillow cover as stiff as starch could make it. These little pillows are not very practical for the inexperienced person, as I learned to my cost. I awakened during the night to find that my pillow had mysteriously disappeared; after searching for it I found it on the floor beside the bed. Again I missed it that night, and again found it on the floor. On the second night I pinned the pillow to the straw bed, and slept undisturbed. Bon Jesus is a remarkable place, not only for the view one has from it over half of Portugal, but for the various means offered for the devotions of pious pilgrims. The last half of the ascent up the mountain is often made by them on their knees climbing up a stairway of four hundred steps. On both sides of this stairway, at short intervals, are small stone chapels, richly decorated both inside and outside with sculptured stone. Each chapel also contains from ten to twenty life-size painted wooden figures in eastern costume, to represent scenes in the life of Christ. On stone tablets above the doors are quotations from the Bible, explaining the figures within. Near the top of the stairway are nine platforms, at short intervals, each surmounted with three stone statues larger than life, representing Old and New Testament characters. Upon all the platforms are stone fountains of running water, engraved with Bible texts. I should add that on the first platform, which is at the beginning of the ascent, is a very large square stone fountain on which are cut representations of the instruments used in the scourging and crucifixion of Christ. People may be seen at all times kneeling before the chapels, which are always open. This stairway is a remarkable construction. Every year several solemn processions ascend the mountain by it.

At the crest of the mountain is the church of Bon Jesus, a modern building of large size and beautiful proportions. It contains many groups of statuary, and the entire ceiling is heavily gilded, on which several sacred scenes are represented in raised stucco-work richly colored. The church is built of granite from the mountain on which it stands, and many of the statues are carved on the spot by Portuguese sculptors, who have great skill in stone work.

Portugal is one of the most beautiful countries in Europe, and possesses many noble buildings reared ages ago and rendered interesting by history and legend; the people, also, are polite and hospitable. I would gladly linger with you amid its lovely scenes, especially at Cintra, near Lisbon, with its palaces and villas embowered in foliage near the blue Atlantic, but we have yet much to see and must therefore continue our journey eastward.

CHAT III.

SWITZERLAND—AUSTRIA—NORWAY.

The Icy Breath of Mountain Glaciers—The Picturesque Costumes of the Tyrol—Ringing Church Bells to Drive Away Thunder—Vienna—The Great Circle of a Noble Street—Leather and Porcelain—Kisses for the Hand—Dazzling Jewels and Splendid Costumes—The Emperor Washing the Feet of Twelve Poor Old Men—With Golden Tray and Pitcher—Mugs and Florins—In the Wine Cellar of Bremen's Town-Hall—How a Bold Doctor of Philosophy Found Himself at the Carousal of the Apostles—Bacchus and Dame Rose—A Story of the Olden Time—At the North Cape—Where the Sun Rises Before it is Fully Set—Hard to Tell When it is Bedtime—The Milk-Fog—Visitors After the Flood.

From the peninsula of Spain and Portugal we will proceed in this evening's chat toward the center of Europe, and stop on the way for a glance at Switzerland. As we approach its lofty mountains we seem to feel its icy breath from the snow-capped peaks, and soon the lovely valley of Chamouni, at the foot of Mt. Blanc, appears before us resting in fresh verdure and enclosed by great glaciers and roaring waterfalls. I remember that I could plainly discern from there foot-weary tourists struggling to get across the *Mer de Glace*, the greatest glacier of the Alps, on the top of the Montanvert, and others venturing down the rough descent called the *Mauvais Pas*, slipped at every step of the way with soft and crumbling soil, and fearing with good reason the

CHAMOUNI.

dreaded avalanche of the earth and stones that sometimes comes rushing down the sides of the mountain. One of the most interesting views of Switzerland is obtained where one beholds the union of the Rhine and the Rhone rivers, not far from the beautiful city of Geneva, on Lake Geneva in Switzerland. The melting glaciers from the Alpine range of mountains are the source of the Rhone river. The waters from the melting snow rush down, forming in places roaring torrents which carry along stones and loose earth, giving to the waters a muddy appearance. These various small streams gradually unite and constitute the river Rhone, which at a short distance from its source mingles with the clear waters of the Rhine. This junction of the two rivers is called the "Meeting of the Waters." The two streams run side by side in the same river bed, each one maintaining its own characteristic color for several miles, and each apparently trying to dominate the other. For a time the clear waters retain their own purity, but as a few drops of muddy water discolor a glassful, so finally these become clouded with the chalky waters of the melting glaciers. At last, however, the clear, crystal waters of the Rhine begin to assert their power, and in another short distance the stream, which has now become a wide river, has taken on a uniform color and flows on and on until, after hundreds of miles, it is lost in the North Sea.

But we are bound still further east this evening and leaving the well-known valleys and glittering peaks of Switzerland, glance a moment at the wild passes and picturesque people of the Tyrol. The Semmering Pass is one of the most remarkable openings in the Tyrol mountains. Here I saw bands of Tyrolese mountaineers, men and women, attired in the national costume which such painters as Debregger have made familiar to many who have been unable to visit that charming country. The women were dressed in black velvet laced bodices with white flowing sleeves, short, bright colored skirts, high top-boots, and jaunty white broad-brimmed straw hats trimmed with long, flowing scarfs of silks of lively hues or with gilt cord and tassels. The men wore white home-spun linen trousers, short and wide; long black or blue knitted stockings; low, heavy shoes with large brass buckles; black velvet tunics confined to the waist with gay scarfs, and their black slouch hats wound around with black and yellow ribbons. They were strolling musicians on their way northward with their Tyrolean airs to give delight to the health and pleasure seekers at the various resorts.

The Tyrolean peasants are a merry, musical, but superstitious race. The mountains are subject to frequent and terrific thunder storms during the months of July and August. At the first sign of an approaching storm, the great bell of the church is rung in the belief that the tempest, if not entirely driven away, is greatly lessened by the sound of the church bell.

From the Tyrol, which is a province of the empire of Austria-Hungary, we pass in a few hours by rail to Vienna, the capital of the empire. Vienna is a beautiful city; the architecture of its buildings is more imposing than that of Paris. There are many magnificent palaces there occupied by the various branches of the royal family. The Ring Strasse, three miles in length, which extends around the old city, is the principal avenue, and on it are some splendid public buildings, many blocks of elegant apartment houses, the Folks Garden, the Stadt Park, and other beautiful parks and gardens. There are six parallel rows of large chestnut trees along this avenue. There is a fine riding track and a carriage-way, two spacious promenades and the sidewalks. There are also long stretches of green lawns with numerous settees beneath the shade of the noble trees, and many handsome cafes and attractive flower-shops continue around the entire circle of the Ring Strasse. This is not only one of the most magnificent, but also one of the most enjoyable promenades of Europe. The daily movement of troops through it adds greatly to the animation it presents.

Vienna is celebrated for its beautiful leather-work. Leather is wrought there in every conceivable way and manufactured into countless useful and ornamental articles. Excellent imitations of metals and fabrics are also made of leather. Nowhere else in Europe are such large collections of glass and porcelain ware to be found as at Vienna. Bohemian glass and Hungarian porcelain are highly prized in all parts of the world. Besides the wares which are particularly Viennese, one may also find there the finest specimens of the famous wares of Sevres.

One who shops in Vienna finds a complimentary greeting in vogue which I have not seen practiced elsewhere. As one enters the shopkeeper exclaims, "Kuss der hand," or, "I kiss your hand," and he repeats the same as one leaves. The servants also use the same expression when they come into the presence of the master or mistress of the house. Before retiring to their rooms at night they again observe this salutation. Hand-kissing in the morning is never forgotten. The coachman gets down from the box of the carriage to kiss the hand of the master, adding a hopeful word about the weather if it be dark or rainy. The collecting boy has the same hand-kissing salutation when he is paid a bill at the door, and the house-servants never forget it when they receive their monthly wages. The *kellvers*, or waiters, at the restaurants always have a polite salutation for those frequenting them. Indeed, as soon as you enter Vienna you become aware that it is a place of extraordinary civilities.

The various nationalities of which the empire is composed add greatly to the public spectacles at Vienna. I have never seen such magnificent toilets, such profusion of jewels, as are seen at Austria's capital on festal occasions. The Polish, Bohemian, Croatian and Hungarian costumes of the government officials are retained in all their splendor of color and decoration. Many of the family jewels of the Viennese are of almost priceless value. They are often heirlooms inherited from several generations back.

There is a curious old religious custom continued at Vienna called the "ceremony of the foot-washing." His Majesty, the Emperor Francis Joseph, has performed the rite for no less than thirty years. The foot-washing is done in the presence of the court and nobility, and is attended with as much pomp as any court ceremonial. Only Austria and Spain now continue this ceremony, which was instituted by the Church in order to teach kings humiliation and their subjection to the Church. The rite takes place in Holy Week, and consists of the emperor pouring a little water over the right foot of twelve old men, in imitation of the example of Christ.

When I witnessed this curious and interesting scene the ceremony took place at eleven o'clock in the morning in the grand hall of ceremonies at the imperial palace. A long table at which the twelve old men were to sit was near the entrance and as handsomely laid as for dinner. The emperor was assisted by the crown prince and several arch-dukes. The old people are selected from the poorest class, and of that class the oldest are chosen. On this occasion the oldest man was ninety-three years old, two were ninety-two, and five were eighty-eight years of age; the others were younger. They were dressed in a plain black costume of the seventeenth century, and wore black silk stockings, and wide, turn-down white collars. They were led into the room by their relatives and friends, and were seated by the court officials, the oldest having the head of the table, and each one having the attendance of a special officer, the relatives and friends standing behind them. The table was strewn with rose leaves, and beneath it were placed brown linen cushions for the feet of the old men to rest upon.

At each plate were a loaf of bread, a napkin, knife, wooden

spoon and fork, a wooden vase filled with flowers, a large white metal mug of wine, and a wooden tankard of beer. The Emperor, in full uniform, came accompanied by officers of his court and assistants, and took his place at the head of the table; then followed twelve officials of the palace, in scarlet and gold uniform, bearing black trays, each containing four dishes of viands, and took their places opposite the old men, who sat along one side of the table. The Emperor cleared the first tray and placed its dishes upon the table before the old man who had the seat of honor. The Crown Prince stood next and served the next old man in turn; and thus each of the old men was served by a grand-duke or some member of the nobility. After the trays were emptied, which was quickly done, the palace guard in full uniform and wearing their high bear-skin hats, entered, bearing trays, on each of which were also four dishes, which were placed before the old men, as were those of the first course, and the third course quickly followed the second. The fourth and last course was the dessert, which included one dozen fine apples, a large piece of cheese, a dish of sweets and a plate of shelled almonds.

When the dinner was ended, although not a morsel had been eaten, the table was taken away, and each old man in turn presented his right foot, which in the meantime had been bared by an attending friend. Then a large golden tray, a golden pitcher and a large napkin were brought and the Emperor knelt upon one knee and poured a little water over the old man's foot and wiped it, and in the same way he washed and wiped one foot of each of the twelve old men. He did not rise to an upright position until he had completed the washing, moving along the row of men upon one knee. The Emperor then rose from his kneeling posture, and the Grand Chamberlain poured water over his hands, which the Emperor wiped with a dry napkin, and the ceremony was finished. Then a court official brought in a large black tray with twelve small bags, a long cord being attached to each bag, which contained thirty silver florins. The Emperor hung a bag upon the neck of each of the old men. This being done, his majesty left the hall.

During the ceremony a chief priest, with twenty assistants, intoned a service and recitations from the gospels, describing the washing of the feet of the disciples by Christ. The ceremony lasted half an hour. All the articles of food and the plates placed before the old men, together with the foot cushions, were packed into baskets and sent to their homes. The tankards and mugs bore appropriate inscriptions with the date of the ceremony. The recipients are permitted to sell their mugs and tankards. The mugs are sold for twenty florins, the tankards for less. Each old man was escorted from the hall by a court official and a friend. The entire ceremony was conducted with great solemnity.

I call to mind here a story of the knights of olden times in Germany, told me in the German language, and which I hope may interest you as much as it did me, even if I give but an imperfect translation of it.

American tourists who visit the north of Germany are pretty sure to go to Bremen, and one of the interesting points to visit there is the wine cellar of the Rathhaus, or town-hall. A German guide offered his services to conduct me through this famous old place, and during the visit of inspection related one of the Rathhaus Keller romances. Somewhere among Shakespeare's sayings the following remark may be found: "Good wine is a good and sociable thing, and everybody can afford for once to allow himself to be inspired by it." My guide probably had heard of this approval of good wine as expressed by the renowned English poet and dramatist, which without doubt brought to his mind the legend related. "The story has been handed down," said the guide, "as it has been told by the hero himself, who was a young student from Leipsig; it runs as follows:

"It was after ten o'clock in the evening when I presented myself at the door of this famous wine-cellar. 'A late hour for admittance to this place,' said the porter at the door, 'for it is about our closing-up time.' However, observing the name of the manager of the wine-rooms on the card giving me permission to enter at that hour, he hesitatingly opened the door a little wider and I went in, remarking in the meantime, 'For me it is never late before twelve o'clock, and after that hour it is early enough in the day for anybody.' The porter asked if I expected any company. I replied, 'No;' and selecting one of the small arched booths of the underground rooms, I laid my hat and cane upon the table, with the intention of carrying out the proposition made to myself to have a little carousal all alone. With a permit in my pocket from one of the senators I had the right to drink a glass from the wine in the Twelve Apostles' cellar, a glass in the Bacchus cellar, and a glass of wine in the Rose cellar. I asked to be conducted at the porter's earliest convenience to the Bacchus cellar. To this the porter replied 'No, that is impossible.' Said he, 'To-day is the first of September, Dame Rose's anniversary. To-night the Twelve Apostles, Bacchus and Dame Rose come down from their stony seats and hold high carnival from midnight till the dawn of day. No man would presume to remain here after midnight.'

"I laughed at the good man's superstition, and replied that I had heard of various ghost-stories, but had never heard of wine ghosts. Then I peremptorily said: 'Look again at the senator's permit; in the name of the Council of Bremen, I command you to open the Bacchus cellar.' We went slowly through several large and dark cellars, with only the light of a lantern to guide us, and at last reached the inner cellar, where a wooden figure of Bacchus sat astride of an immense wine-cask.

'Good heavens!' cried the porter, 'do n't you see how the old fellow rolls his eyes and shakes his feet? He is getting ready to come down now. Let us be off.' 'Why, man, it is only the shadow of our flickering light that gives you this impression,' said I. However, we left the cellar, and the porter locked the big oak door with a nervous quickness, but not until I had drank a glass of the old Bacchus wine drawn from the sample barrel. 'Here, old porter, take a glass at my expense,' said I, 'it will give you a little courage.' 'God preserve me from drinking a drop of it this night!' he exclaimed.

"We wandered on a little farther by the dim light of our lantern and came to the Apostles' cellar. The rusty lock of the heavy door gave an unearthly grating sound as the key slowly turned in it; the door opened, creaking on its heavy hinges, and there stood the statues of the twelve Apostles in their garb of hewn-out stone, high up in the niches in the wall, and beneath them twelve great casks of wine. 'I must have a glass of wine from this cellar to drink the health of these antiques,' said I. The porter fairly trembled at my light remark, and replied, 'Good sir, do n't you know that you are tempting the devil? This is the night when all the wine ghosts come down from their places to have their yearly carousal. It is now nearly midnight. I have never known of a man staying here on the first of September until the stroke of midnight. I must go, and I cannot answer for your safety if you persist in remaining much longer.' 'But you cannot go until you have taken me to the Rose cellar,' I exclaimed. We passed quickly on and came to the *Sub Rosa* cellar. 'What a monster cask of wine, and every glass of it is worth a gold piece!' I said. I read upon it the date of 1615. 'Fill me a glass from the sample barrel quickly. I must drink old Dame Rose's health before the clock strikes twelve, and then, good porter, you can go, and I will stay in the Rose cellar for a little time.' 'Oh, no! that is utterly impossible; I should lose my place were I to leave the door unlocked,' declared the old man.

"I followed in the wake of the dim light and went back to the place where I had left my hat and cane. 'But before you go, good man,' said I, 'give me a couple of bottles of the vintage of 1718.' He did as I requested, saying, 'I cannot leave you all night alone in the cellar; you will be frightened to death with the doings among the ghosts.' 'But you know I have permission to remain here all night, and I intend to stay. So good night, my friend, and don't worry any more about me. Lock the door of the outer room and take the key with you, and I will draw the inside bolt on the door of this room. I want no intruders to-night. Leave me a half dozen candles; and I want nothing more.' He complied and then went hesitatingly toward the door, opened and closed it slowly, remaining inside apparently to give me time to change my intentions if I wished to do so. But I was immovable in my purpose. At last he went out, leisurely locking the street door, and then calling to me from outside he said: 'My friend, I am sure I shall find you dead from fright when I return at six o'clock in the morning.'

"I examined my quarters carefully and found no other door than the one through which I had entered, and upon the table were two bottles of real Johannes wine marked 1718.

"I heard the cathedral clock strike twelve, and I had already drank my sixth glass of wine, when the thought occurred to me that there is a time when wine will go to one's head, and I was just wondering whether I should be able to finish my two bottles when I fancied that I heard a heavy door slowly opening on its creaking hinges, and in another moment I was sure I heard the echoing sound of the heavy tread of footsteps. I remembered that the outside door was locked and that the porter had taken the key with him, and I knew the door of the room in which I was, was also locked, and besides I had drawn the bolt inside. So I quieted myself with the thought that there would be no admittance, under any circumstances, to the room this night.

"At this moment, and to my utter astonishment, the door opened without being unlocked or unbolted, and I saw two men standing in the door-way dressed in antique costume, saluting each other. They advanced slowly into the room, and taking off their swords and hats, hung them on large hooks on the wall. They then seated themselves at the table where I was, apparently not observing my presence. I was about to speak and make myself known, when four more unbidden guests entered the open door, saying, 'Good morning, gentlemen of the Rhine. Where is the old servant Johannes? Is he still sleeping at his post?' 'Yes, he is in the church-yard fast asleep. I'll just ring him up,' said the man nearest me, who, taking up a huge bell, rang it long and loud. The summons was quickly answered by a hollow-eyed old man, who appeared at the door, yawning and rubbing his eyes, having a large basket filled with bottles on his arm. 'Hallo, old Johannes, you are a sluggard this time; step along a little more lively,' said the man who had rung the bell. The old servant—for it was he who answered the summons of the bell—replied that he had forgotten that it was the first of September; that since they had paved the church-yard anew he did not hear so well as formerly what was going on over his head. 'But,' said he, 'where are the rest of you? You are only six, and old Dame Rose is not here yet.' 'Well,' said the one they called Judas, 'put down the bottles; we must wet our lips; give us the glasses and then go over there,' pointing to the door, 'and call up the rest of your number, who are still sleeping in the wine-casks.'

"At this moment a great commotion was heard outside the door, and old Johannes cried out, 'Here come Dame Rose and her lover, the jolly old Bacchus.' What a sight! There was the wooden Bacchus, and the mammoth cask of wine that I had seen in the Rose Cellar and which they called Dame Rose, followed closely by four lively old fellows swinging cocked hats in their hands. 'At last, we are all here,' said one of the party of stone statues, 'and as for Dame Rose, she looks just as she did fifty years ago. But how is this? We are thirteen at the table. Who is the stranger among us? How happens it that he is here?'

"Aware that I was an unbidden guest among them, I at once briefly explained my presence. I said that I was simply a Doctor of Philosophy from Leipsig, and that at present I was living at the Hotel Frankfurt, in Bremen. 'But what brought you here on this particular night, good sir?' inquired another. 'You know that you do not belong to the noble society of two hundred years ago?' 'Of that,' I replied, 'I am perfectly well aware, for I did not live two hundred years ago. But your noble selves have come to me to-night; I did not make the trespass upon you. When I came here I found no company. The good old porter of the Rathhaus Keller locked the door and took the key with him! 'Tell me,' asked Bacchus, 'what are you doing in the Rathhaus Keller at this late hour of the night? The world's people in Bremen are never out of their homes at midnight.' 'Your excellency,' said I, 'there is good reason for my being here at this time. I am a friend of good old Rhine wine, and have obtained permission from one of the noble senators of Bremen to come here and get some to my taste. I have chosen this night, because I have read some very interesting accounts about the carousals held here on the night of the first of September by some of the distinguished men of the olden times, and I desired to make some scientific observations.' 'Ha! ha!' laughed Bacchus, 'that is well enough; you shall have a little dance with us to-night.'

"I now began to look around me, and to observe the company. There were some of the stone statues of the twelve apostles I had seen standing in their niches as I passed through the Apostles' cellar: Bacchus in his wooden body, and Dame Rose, her body a great wine-cask, was standing upon two tiny little feet near by, her coquettish face peeping out from the upper end of the cask, with the copper rose of the *Sub-Rosa* cellar hanging on the front of it. All were in a jolly mood. They laughed and talked with each other in unearthly tones. I judged from their conversation that they were accustomed to have a reunion every year, and that they had been meeting together in this way for a hundred years or more.

"They told stories over their glasses of wine—kept continually replenished by the old servant Johannes. The stories related by them referred to historic and social events of their times. One of the ghosts told how some of the old Bremen families used to come to the Rathhaus Keller at five o'clock in the forenoon, grandmothers, wives and children included, and remain until eight o'clock in the evening, at which time the cellar was always closed. 'Yes,' said Dame Rose, 'those were good old times, when we drunk only pure Rhine wines; we did n't have this miserable stuff now called tea and coffee, and such beverages as are drunk now-a-days.'

"The carousal was waxing more lively, when suddenly a new apparition made its appearance. All voices were hushed. Even Bacchus turned pale. The intruder took a seat by me. I whispered to a ghost close by me and asked who this last comer was. He replied, 'Do n't you see, it is the devil himself! He always comes in at our anniversary meetings and attempts to disturb us.' A glass of wine was set before him and he remained quiet.

"After several old-time songs had been sung at the request of Dame Rose, she winked at me and said, 'Now, doctor, it is your turn; as this is your first appearance among us, you must give us a song which never has been sung before.' I attempted to excuse myself on the ground that I could neither sing nor make verse. 'No excuses are accepted here,' she blandly replied. 'You have come unbidden to us to-night, and you must join in our exercises. Come, sir, we are waiting for you.' Tremblingly I arose, and by some happy inspiration the following words were put into my mouth :

"On the beautiful Rhine, where grows our vine,
There grows our golden, luscious wine ;
Yonder it grows on our German coast,
And gives us all the never-dying toast,
Rhine wine, Rhine wine,
Always in tune and in time."

"The ghostly company laughed heartily, and Bacchus exclaimed, 'What a noble addition the doctor will be to our choice spirits ! We all hope he may join our merry circle soon.' In my soul I could not agree with him, for I had not yet seen enough of life. But under the circumstances I did not wish to discuss the subject.

"They now commenced to arrange for a dance. Bacchus was the leader of the party. He called to me and said : 'Of course, doctor, you know music. We shall depend on you for this occasion. Get upon that cask of wine and beat the drum for our dance.' I obeyed. A step-ladder was necessary to aid me in reaching the top of the large wine cask. When seated, my head just touched the timbers of the vaulted roof. All was proceeding well, when suddenly I saw the heavy beams over my head part, and I with my drum flew like an arrow out into the open air. I said to myself, 'Good-bye, good-bye to this life ; these accursed ghosts have entered my name in their death-book.'

"The first sensation I experienced afterward was the touch of the Rathhaus Keller porter on my shoulder. Hearing his morning salutation and inquiry respecting my welfare, I began to rub my eyes and look about me, and getting up on my feet, I found that I had become intoxicated, and had fallen from the bench upon the stone floor. As there was no evidence of my having had company in the night, I concluded that my solitary carousal was only a dream. But I could not convince myself that the strone statues had not actually come down from their places—so strong was the impression on my mind that the night's adventure was a reality—until I made the round of all the cellars I had visited the evening before, and saw for myself that the stone figures were all in their places."

From Bremen I proceeded to Norway across the Baltic sea. The scenery of this most northern country in Europe is highly romantic and beautiful; the shores are steep and rocky, broken by deep, narrow bays and straits, called fiords. But what most interested me, and I doubt not would interest you as well, is the view of the midnight sun from the North Cape. It is a most wonderful spectacle to see the sun just dipping its lower edge for a moment behind the horizon in the west and then coming almost immediately to view again on the other side in the east, rising even before it has fully set. This phenomenon is caused by the fact that the earth's circle from east to west is so short that the sun is visible the greater part of the time.

The North Cape is the most northern point on the Continent of Europe; until within a few years it was scarcely known to the general European tourist. It is a precipitous rock rising out of the sea to a height of twelve hundred feet.

A German friend who has been twice to the North Cape says no more wonderful journey can be made than the one from Trondhjem to the Cape. He was fourteen days in making the excursion, without once seeing the darkness of night during all that time. His disposition to sleep seemed to have disappeared with the night, he said, and it was only when the body and mind became really fatigued that he was able to fall asleep. Not far from the Cape is a natural tunnel through the entire mountain. In passing that point the ship was stopped, and one could look through the tunnel and plainly see the water on the opposite side of the Cape. A peculiar fog settles over this point, called the milk-fog, because of its opaqueness and milk color.

The long winter of the northern regions follows almost suddenly on the disappearance of the sunlight, but the absence of solar light is compensated for in a measure by the frequent appearance of the *aurora borealis*, or northern lights, which give light enough to allow the ordinary avocations of life to be carried on without artificial illumination.

This is an interesting subject for a more thorough study.

In passing, I would say that I remember to have heard that one of the early Swedish historians claims that after the deluge Sweden was the first country to be inhabited west of the Mediterranean Sea. The historian records that Magog, son of Japheth, with a few followers, came to Gothland, in Sweden, eighty-eight years after the flood and established a permanent settlement, and that two hundred and twenty-six years thereafter a direct descendant of that colony commenced the building of the city of Upsal. We might ask ourselves why did Magog and his followers forsake the blue skies and balmy air of a southern climate for the deep snows and biting frosts of an inhospitable one!

But as not a trace of this ancient city is left upon which to build a description, we can only consider the story as an amusing legend.

CHAT IV.

GREECE—ATHENS.

Ancient Greeks whose Names and Deeds are still Cherished —A Nation that Hundreds of Years of Subjection could not Destroy—Building out of Ruins—Americans who Taught the Children of Greece—A Monument more Enduring than the Parthenon—Where the Temple Stones were Quarried—The Preacher on Mars's Hill—Mountains and Houses of Marble—The Salt of Friendship—The Bride's Dower-Chest—A Mountainous Weather-Prophet —The English General and his Wife's Letter—A Weekly Epistle for Thirty Years—At Last too Late—Christmas and New Year's Twice in Twelve Days—The Story of the Labyrinth—The Galley with the Black Sails—A Brave Prince and a Slain Monster—Digging Down to the Old City of Troy.

Leaving the north of Europe for the south of the Continent, our chat this evening is about Athens, the capital of Greece, one of the oldest as well as the most widely celebrated cities in the world.

Something is known of the classic antiquity of Athens the world over; and without doubt, ancient Athens was the birthplace of modern civilization. It was the home of classic and philosophic lore. Plato, Socrates, Demosthenes, Solon, Plutarch, Pericles, and many other celebrated philosophers, poets and statesmen of Greece established by their teachings and example the public opinion and laws which gave such power to the

THE ACROPOLIS, ATHENS.

genius of the Greeks and made them the greatest in intellectual influence the world has yet seen. Among those noble men there was one Diogenes, who adopted a peculiarly original method for teaching the principle of truth. For example, he went about the city one day with a lighted lantern in his hand, and when asked for an explanation, he replied he was seeking to find an honest man.

Many of the philosophical maxims taught by those wise men of Greece have come down through generations until they have reached even to our own times, and apply to the present age as well as to the days of ancient Greece. The Greeks are a noble race, and they have good reason to be proud.

Although Greece had groaned under the domination of the Turks for more than four hundred years, the nation did not lose its identity. The Turks and Greeks never intermarried, nor do they intermarry in these days. They have no more common cause in life now than they had then. It is only within the last sixty years that Greece has freed herself from the yoke of the Ottoman power.

At last, in the year 1827, when the diminished and impoverished Grecian Empire was able to raise once more its banner of freedom, they found their once beautiful Athens, the queen city of the Mediterranean, in ruins, with scarcely a score of good buildings remaining.

It was three years after this time that the late Dr. J. J. Robertson and the late Rev. Dr. John H. Hill with his wife went to Athens with the intention of devoting themselves to missionary work. Dr. and Mrs. Hill had already been at work in Smyrna, Asia Minor, for a short time in behalf of Christian education for the benefit of the Greeks and Armenians living there, but they saw a larger field for their labors in Greece. On their arrival in Athens they found only about twenty houses standing, not one of which was really comfortable for a home. However, they were permitted by the newly-established Greek government to open a school for little girls in their own small house. This was done principally by the aid of Mrs. Emma Willard of Troy, New York, who, from the beginning of the independence of the Greeks, took an earnest interest in the work of primary education among the children, and was the first person to give a helping hand to that object. At the urgent request of Mrs. Willard a small sum of money was raised in Troy, I think among the Episcopal churches only, and sent to the Rev. Messrs. Hill and Robertson, for the purpose of establishing a small school for girls.

The school work commenced under many embarrassments; but as the population became more settled, the school increased in numbers, and during the last years of Dr. Hill's life it numbered over six hundred pupils, both boys and girls.

Dr. Hill was ordained minister in the Episcopal church in the year 1830; he was already forty years of age. Soon thereafter with his wife he left America to go to the Orient with the intention of devoting themselves to the missionary service. They worked for their beloved cause in Greece more than fifty-two years. Dr. Hill died at his post of service in 1882, and Mrs. Hill followed her loving husband to her long rest a few years later. They were the first missionaries sent by the Episcopal church to foreign lands.

The following words addressed to Mrs. Hill by a Greek statesman express the approval of her work among the Greeks and the high esteem in which she was held: "Lady, you are erecting in Athens a monument more enduring and more noble than yonder temple," pointing to the Parthenon as he spoke. And they were prophetic words.

Dr. and Mrs. Hill did not go to an idolatrous people to begin their life-work. The Greeks had long years before come out from the darkness of paganism. They had a national Christian church ; they had the bible, the ministry, the sacraments, and the liturgy, which they had maintained through the hundreds of years of their subjection to the Turks ; but while they were heroes in courage they were weak in numbers and in destitute condition, and had fallen into some superstitions. They gladly, however, accepted the material aid which came from the American missionary society, and the educational advantages personally offered by Dr. and Mrs. Hill.

Dr. Hill's system of instruction was approved by many of the Greeks, and some of the leading families sent children to the school. It can be said that large numbers of the representative men and women of Athens, and of the neighboring islands, who have come into public life during the last twenty-five years, received their primary education in this American Missionary School, and in many cases in the schools established some years later by other devoted and useful American missionaries of the Congregationalists and Baptists, all equally anxious to aid the progress of Greece.

Dr. and Mrs. Hill passed sixty-one years together, side by side, in their life work.

The ancient Greek temples, whose ruins are still standing, many in a fair state of preservation, were built three to seven hundred years B. C., and even in their ruins may be seen evidences of magnificent marble structures. The quarries on Mount Pentelicus, from which the marble was obtained for the wonderful edifices, remain as they were left by the ancients. The quarry which furnished the marble for the Parthenon, the most famous temple of all time and dedicated to the goddess Minerva, is still to be seen. Even a section or drum of one of the columns, apparently discarded on account of some flaw in the marble, remains there half embedded in the earth a little way down the mountain.

St. Paul was the first teacher of Christianity in Athens ; and one of the most interesting places in the city to visit is the Areopagus, or in English Mars's Hill, this appellation having been given it, according to the traditional account, because the god Mars was the first person tried by a court of justice upon this hill.

In Acts XVII. mention is made of St. Paul preaching to the curious and superstitious Athenians. The populace of Athens, who went daily to the Agora, or market place, which was near the foot of Mars's Hill, to learn the news of the day, heard that a strange man had come among them who pretended to have a new doctrine of religion, and that he had asked permission of the city authorities to speak to the people from Mars's Hill, the place where all public speaking was done.

When the crowd had assembled the apostle said that he had observed altars erected to Fame, Modesty, Energy, Persuasion and Piety, and that he had also seen an altar dedicated to the unknown God at a point near the sea, and this altar he wished to dedicate anew to the God he came to preach. Thus St. Paul sowed the first seed of Christianity among the Greeks, which indeed did take root and has given forth a great harvest.

The Athens of to-day is a beautiful and growing city; it has more marble buildings in proportion to its size than any other city in Europe. It has mountains of marble at its very doors.

The Greeks are a very social people and hospitably inclined. Among their many agreeable domestic customs is that of offering salt to a guest immediately after sitting down to a meal; its acceptance gives proof of true friendship.

Another very good as well as a practical custom is that of providing the marriage portion for a daughter. The collection of a maiden's dower is begun while she is a child, as was customary with the Greeks in ancient times. The Greek maidens of all classes, even to the poorest peasant's daughter, are sure

MARS HILL, ATHENS.

to have a marriage dower. Among the lower classes and the peasantry it is effected in this wise. As soon as the little girl is beyond the dangers of infancy, the prudent mother buys a wooden box, which is painted red and yellow and bears the name of the child upon it; it may be large or small, according to circumstances; in this box the god-mother's gift is placed and any others that may be bestowed on the occasion of the child's birth. On every succeeding birth-day anniversary, some useful articles contributed by parents or friends are added to the contents of the box in the name of the little girl; it may be a gold or silver coin, a silver spoon, or a small piece of linen made by the mother or grandmother. These contributions to the dower box are carefully treasured until the girl marries, when the well-filled chest is given to the bride.

The scenery about Athens is mountainous, very picturesque and beautiful. Mts. Pentelicus, Parnes and Hymettus are famous.

The Athenians have a very significant little rhyme velating to the latter mountain, which serves them as a weather prophecy; it runs as follows:

"Old Hymettus, Hymettus,
You'll surely wet us,
When the clouds come down
To weave you a crown."

An affecting incident and also a very interesting chapter in the experience and devotion of a husband and wife, showing the maintenance of conjugal affection by correspondence for a long period of years, may not be inappropriate to relate at this time. The closing scene of this story occurred while the writer was a temporary resident in Athens.

During the latter part of the struggle of the Greeks for indedependence against the Turkish domination, an English general volunteered to go to the aid of the oppressed people. At the end of the war the English general had so ardently espoused the Greek cause that he continued to remain in the country and to render such aid to the newly-formed government as he might be able to give. Accordingly, he sent for his wife, who was in England, to come to the more genial climate of the plains of Attica.

In due time Lady —— went to Athens. After two or three years' residence there, she became somewhat discontented with the unsettled and half-formed social situation at the new capital and decided to return to England for a few months' visit. This she did unattended by the general, as the military situation at that time required his constant service, and it was not convenient for him to leave his post. So the good lady packed up her boxes and bundles and went home, with the intention of returning the following year.

Months passed on and Lady —— did not find the occasion to go back to Athens, always hoping that the general would seek a leave of absence after his many years of active service in a foreign military life, and go to England, when she would with pleasure return with him.

Years rolled on, and the devoted couple were growing old separated far from each other. They had not met since the day of the good lady's departure from Athens. The weekly letter, continued by this time for a period of nearly thirty years between the two, had never been intermitted.

At last the general was laid low on his death-bed. He had reached the age of one hundred years, of which fifty had been devoted to service in Greece. On the last day of his life, it chanced that the usual weekly epistle came from Lady ——, which was shown to the dying man by his valet. The general asked, "From whom comes the letter?" The answer was, "From Lady ——." To which he replied, "Too late, too late," and soon he was no more.

The Greeks maintain the ancient form of reckoning the days of the month. There is a difference by twelve days between the old and new system of counting time. Foreigners residing in Greece must familiarize themselves with the difference of date, else untold embarrassments may occur. Consequently Christmas and New Year's days—they being the principal holidays celebrated in common—are repeated. Two Christmas days and two New Year's,—four holidays within twenty days!

As one may easily suppose, Athens abounds with historic spots and is rich beyond almost any other place in the memory of great events and numerous legends and traditions. One of the most interesting is the legend of the good heart and the bravery of Theseus, one of the kings of ancient Athens. It runs as follows: Minos, King of the Island of Crete, opened a warfare on the Athenians, because, as was alleged, his son had been betrayed and killed while on a visit to Athens. At the earnest entreaty of Minos, the gods brought upon the plain of Attica all kinds of plagues, sickness among the people, sterility of the lands, and terrible drought.

At last by the oracle of Apollo it was announced to the Athenians that the anger of the gods could only be appeased by making peace with Minos. Accordingly messengers from Athens were sent to him to sue for mercy and peace. King Minos consented to cease warring with the Athenians on the condition that they should pay him a yearly tribute of seven maidens of tender age.

The condition was accepted, the warfare ceased, and the plain of Attica blossomed into prosperity again. These young people, according to the tradition, were sent to the Island of Crete and there placed in a dreadful enclosure called the Labyrinth, which was a prison of dark and endless corridors, where lived the fabulous monster called the Minotaur. As the imprisoned ones never found their way out, it was supposed that they were devoured by the Minotaur.

The time arrived for paying the tribute for the third year. Theseus, son of Ægeus, King of Athens, by this time had come to young manhood, and would soon, by virtue of his parentage, be among the aspirants for the throne of Athens. He bethought himself of a means to satisfy Minos without permitting this dreadful human sacrifice.

The doomed ones were chosen by lot. What parent could of his own free choice consent to give up a beloved child to such a fate! Theseus begged the privilege of being one of the victims, in the hope of finding some way to slay the Minotaur.

Theseus begged Ægeus, his father, and friends not to be disconsolate, assuring them that he would come back and bring the full number of his companions with him. The ship bearing the victims departed as usual with black sails, but Theseus promised that if he returned victorious he would hoist white sails as a signal of triumph.

The day arrived for the departure of this dreadful sacrifice. Theseus took his little band of thirteen unhappy young creatures to a temple on the beach and offered the god Apollo a branch of an olive tree with fourteen bands of white linen upon it. When he had finished his prayer, they went directly to the sea and embarked upon the vessel. The litttle galley was made ready at once, and went out of port carrying the black sail.

When they arrived at Crete, Ariadne, daughter of Minos, was on the shore watching the coming of the Athenian bark with the doomed youth on board. Smitten by the bravery and beauty of the young Greek, she fell in love with him and wished to save him from the dreadful fate before him. She gave him a ball of white linen thread as a clue and told him where to place it on going into the Labyrinth, and how to let it follow him, and if he succeeded in overcoming the Minotaur he would be able to retrace his steps and thus find his way out.

Theseus with his young companions entered the Labyrinth and after winding about its gloomy mazes encountered the ferocious monster. After a severe contest the Minotaur was overcome and killed by the valor of Theseus, and the brave youth with the group of maidens, following the unwound thread, retraced their way and came out of the Labyrinthian prison unharmed.

They returned at once to their vessel, and embarked, setting sail for Athens. As they approached home, Theseus forgot to raise the white sail, and the old father, Ægeus, who had been watching from the headland of Sunium with an aching heart for the return of the little bark, espied it in the distance with the black sail. Supposing his son had been killed, and not being able to bear the torture of grief, he threw himself into the sea and was drowned. Hence the name of the Ægean sea.

The vessel came into port; but Theseus looked anxiously in vain among the eager crowd for his father. Ægeus being dead Theseus became king of Athens, and proved a good and powerful ruler.

One of the most remarkable men now living at Athens is Dr. Schliemann. All who are interested in the great legend of the Trojan and the beautiful poem of Homer called the Iliad, describing the siege of Troy, must be attracted by the name of this enthusiastic searcher among the ruins of ancient times. Dr. Schliemann, a German by birth, but an American citizen from preference, and a Greek by adoption, after many years of hard work in making excavations on the site of ancient Troy—at his own expense—and publishing the results of his labors, has so clearly demonstrated the reality of the events described and the characters of the Iliad that he has brought them to our very doors, as it were, and made the pre-historic times appear as if of our day. Even the young student may read Dr. Schliemann's works with great interest.

Mrs. Schliemann, an Athenian lady, has been an earnest co-worker with her husband in his literary labors as well as in the actual work of excavations. With her own hands she has unearthed some exceedingly valuable specimens of pottery and other articles of very ancient date.

CHAT V.

TURKEY.

The Sea where Helle Sank—The Swimmer of the Ancient Tale—The Turkish Capital—Visiting a Harem—The Favorite Daughter of the Grand Vizier—Her Gorgeous Rooms—A Picturesque Costume—The Singing of Slave Girls—Sipping Coffee from Jeweled Cups of Gold—A Circassian Princess—Diamond Earrings that Rested on Her Shoulders—The Prime Minister's Idea of America—The Bedroom of the Princess—A Hospitable Invitation—On the Bosphorus in a Graceful Caique—The Sultan's Palace—His Bathroom of Alabaster and Silver—The Queen Mother—How She Goes Boating—The Sultan's Birthday Present—In a Peacock Garden—Ordering a Palace—Turkish Homes—The Terraced Bosphorus—An American's Noble Gift—In the Mosque—How the Women Gossip on the Ferry Boats—Reckoning Time.

We sailed from Athens for Constantinople. The track of our steamer lay through the Greek archipelago, sometimes called the Ægean Sea. It is thickly studded with beautiful islands celebrated in classical history and rich with legendary lore. We passed through the Hellespont, a narrow strait now called the Dardanelles. It connects the Ægean Sea with the Sea of Marmora. The Hellespont received its name from the following circumstances: A young Greek girl named Helle and her brother Phrixus were persecuted by their stepmother Ino ages ago, according to the legend. They fled from their home in Thessaly on a golden ram given them by the god Mercury. This valuable animal was able to fly through the air, and in this way he safely bore the two children as far as the Hellespont. But when they were passing over that strait Helle fell into the sea and was drowned. Hence it was called the sea of Helle or Hellespont.

This strait is also famous on account of Hero and Leander. The former was a lovely young priestess who lived at Sestos, opposite Abydos, where Leander lived. Often he swam the boisterous strait at night to visit her, guided by the torch she kept lit on the top of a tower. But one stormy night Leander was drowned, and when at daybreak Hero saw his corpse floating on the waves she threw herself into the sea from the tower and perished with him. From the Dardanelles one may also see the famous plains where Troy once stood, and Mount Ida, the scene of so many interesting legends.

The sail across the sea of Marmora brought us in sight of Constantinople. It is a great and celebrated city, beautifully situated on the Sea of Marmora and the strait called the Bosphorus, which leads to the Black Sea. The prospect is unsurpassed for loveliness as one sails towards the city on a pleasant day.

Many gilded domes, minarets, kiosks and palaces surrounded with gardens on the hillsides down to the water's edge line both shores of the Bosphorus.

While at Constantinople I was invited to visit the harem or ladies' rooms of the establishment of the Sultan's Grand Vizier or Prime Minister. I was fortunately accompanied by a European lady, the wife of the court physician, who kindly offered her services as interperter. We were received at the entrance of the palace by a half-dozen slave girls prettily dressed in bright colors, who escorted us through several long corridors, the walls of which were faced with oriental amber-colored

THE GOLDEN HORN, FROM PERA.

alabaster, while the vaulted ceilings were supported by columns of prophyry, verd antique and other beautiful marbles. We were conducted up an alabaster staircase into a large room furnished with low and luxurious divans on all sides covered with rich Persian stuffs; beautiful velvet and gold embroidered cushions were spread on the floor to serve also as seats.

Immediately after our entrance other gaily attired slave-girls brought nargalees or waterpipes, with amber and jeweled mouthpieces, which were offered us. This politeness we were obliged to decline, saying that American ladies had not yet accustomed themselves to the habit of smoking. We then went to another room, where the windows were protected by finely-carved wooden lattice-work, as indeed are all the windows in the women's apartments of a Turkish house. Here we were served with delicious black coffee in tiny golden cups ornamented with precious stones, which we accepted with pleasure. From this room we were conducted through magnificent arched marble halls furnished with costly rugs and divans upholstered with rich embroideries, into the salon of the eldest daughter of the grand vizier. A curtain of cloth of gold was raised; the favorite daughter, surrounded by a half-dozen attendants gorgeously dressed in silks and literally covered with flashing jewels, received us at the entrance and invited us to be seated on a divan. There were beautiful divans on all sides of the room, which with the floor cushions were covered with crimson velvet and gold embroideries and trimmed with golden cord and tassels.

Upon the wall was a life-sized portrait of the Sultan, the only picture in the palace. There were books in French and English strewn around upon the divans. It is said that this princess is the only Turkish woman who could speak or read in any other than her own language; but I cannot vouch for the truth of this statement.

The princess received us most graciously, addressing us in English. Her toilet was in accordance with the national costume, consisting of wide pantaloons of blue silk gathered at the ankles, and a short tunic of crimson velvet embroidered and fringed with gold thread and seed pearls, and confined at the waist with a golden girdle from which long golden cords and tassels were suspended. The sleeves were slashed to the shoulders, displaying magnificent armlets of jewels worn above the elbows. Her fez or head-dress was of crimson velvet ornamented on one side with an aigrette of precious stones in crescent form ; a pair of yellow kid slippers completed her toilet.

The princess called our attention to some of her books, telling us that she read them with much pleasure. At a signal, her slave attendants commenced singing, accompanying themselves with most novel-looking instruments ; but if we thought the music strange and perhaps inharmonious, we did not say so. These slave girls were about the same age as the princess ; they were born in the palace, and had been given to her in their infancy, having been trained to do her bidding and to entertain their mistress.

After a time a small, low, round table was brought in, upon which were placed golden cups filled with black coffee, and cushions were arranged by it as seats for us. This was a signal that our visit with the princess was about to terminate. The custom among the Turkish ladies is to offer coffee, cigarettes, and nargalees to visitors on their entrance, and again on their departure.

We had a most agreeable conversation while sipping our coffee from the jeweled cups.

When we had finished, the princess asked us if we would like to be presented to her mother. Accepting her invitation, we were conducted to that lady's apartments by another half-dozen beautifully-dressed slave girls and attended by a eunuch attired in a gorgeous uniform of scarlet and gold, decorated with jewels. The noble lady was a beautiful blonde Circassian woman. She received us reclining upon a rich divan, with a gilt and alabaster table close at hand, supplied with perfumed cigarettes, several jeweled amber mouth-pieces, and a golden candlestick holding a lighted taper. Coffee and cigarettes were immediately offered us.

This princess was arrayed in a flowing white muslin gown, confined at the waist with a golden cord and tassels of seed pearls. Her ear-rings were in the form of the fuchsia, a beautiful drooping flower, and composed entirely of diamonds cut in varied shapes to represent the flower. They were so long that they literally rested upon her shoulders. Among the Turkish women it is considered a high compliment if their articles of dress are remarked upon and admired, and on this occasion indeed we did not forbear admiring these exquisite jewels. She took them from her ears and allowed us to examine them at our leisure.

After a few informal compliments had been exchanged, we were invited into the music room, where a dozen magnificently-attired girls as black as night gave us a repetition of the same kind of music we had already heard. When the music was finished the grand vizier himself came into the room, and through the interpreter asked if we had gas in America to illuminate our houses. He said he thought our country was yet too young to have such luxuries! He desired to know if there were many white people in America. He seemed to have the idea that the inhabitants were mostly Indians. We gave him some points of instruction, and among others told him we had a railroad from the Atlantic to the Pacific oceans about four thousand miles long. I doubt if he really believed our story. He probably thought we were talking in hyperbole, or exaggerated language, such as orientals love to indulge in.

We were then conducted to the bedroom of the princess, the grand vizier accompanying us. The principal furniture in this room was an unusually large bedstead made of gilded wood, and built up so high from the floor that in order to reach it two steps had been constructed the length of the bedstead, over which velvet was laid. The bed was covered with a white counterpane fringed with gold thread ; the pillow cases were also embroidered at the open ends with the same rich thread, and both of these articles could be washed. There was no other furniture in the room except a long divan, luxurious floor cushions and beautiful softly-tinted rugs.

In due time we indicated that the limit of our visit had expired. The hospitable vizier replied that he would assign to us an apartment which we were at liberty to occupy as long as we might desire, and he would send for our friends and clothes. We declined his polite invitation, and with the exchange of many compliments we took our leave.

On descending the staircase we found at the entrance a magnificent caique, or row boat, manned by a dozen caique-men in holiday attire. This graceful, fairy-like boat was furnished with crimson velvet cushions trimmed with gold fringe and tassels, and large squares of fringed velvet were thrown over the sides ; the floor of the caique was carpeted with the same rich stuff ; there was a large gilt crescent at the prow, and, in our honor, an American flag was at the stern. This caique was placed at our service.

We could not resist the temptation to take a little turn on the Bosphorus, and we went to see the sultan's palace. This building is of white marble, with doors hung on silver hinges and their trimmings of the same metal. The windows were also ornamented with silver. The bath-room was indeed a marvel of beauty ; it was about twenty feet square with no other visible material in its construction than alabaster and silver. The bath fountain in the center of the room was of solid silver, from which issued jets of tepid perfumed water. The necessary bathing accessories were of silver, and snow-white linen. We were told that on the site of this bath-house once stood a beautiful palace occupied at times by the sultan, and that because one of his favorite Circassian wives died in the palace he caused it to be taken down and the bath-palace built in its place.

The mother of the sultan holds the place of honor over all the women of the sultan's household. She has her own palace, and an immense income called "Slipper money;" she also has a retinue of one hundred and fifty slaves at her command. She is called the *sultana valide*, or queen mother, the highest title given to a Turkish woman. When she drives out she has a suite of thirty girls gorgeously arrayed in bright clothes and fine jewels, and an escort of a dozen black eunuchs, attired in scarlet and gold, mounted on splendid Arabian horses.

When the *sultana valide* makes an excursion on the Bosphorus she goes in an imperial caique. The twenty caiquemen are dressed in white silk shirts and trousers, and wear the red fez with a long blue silk tassel. She reclines under a canopy of crimson velvet with white golden fringe. The caique is white, ornamented with traceries of gold and crimson. Five imperial caiques carrying ladies of honor attend her.

It is said that seven thousand people daily eat bread and salt from the sultan's store at a cost of millions a year. The sultana's yearly birth-day present to the sultan is a young and beautiful Circassian slave-girl.

We also made a visit to the sultan's peacock aviary. This is a large garden surrounded by a high wall, and contains several enchanting little kiosks, besides a number of unique fountains. These kiosks are the favorite resorts of the ladies of the harem, where they are served with coffee and sugared fruits, and from whence they observe the graceful movements of the bright-plumaged peacocks. There were nearly a hundred of these birds of all sizes in the garden: the ground was literally carpeted with the fallen feathers. We were allowed to gather a handful of these brilliant plumes.

The sultan has many palaces on the Bosphorus. On a certain occasion he desired a new palace; it was ordered in the month of February and finished in the following June. He has only to command and his wish is law.

There is no family among the Turks as we know home life. The women are not confined to their homes by domestic duties and responsibilities. The details of the house are arranged by a steward, who cares for the entire establishment. The women are free to visit from house to house in their own vicinity at their pleasure. With a small calico bag containing necessary articles, and two or three little children, boys and girls, tugging at her skirts, and dressed like the mother, she goes about the neighborhood visiting friends and remaining as long as she may find it agreeable. The little boys are taken from their mother at the age of ten years and placed at school or in the military barracks, and a few years later are put into the service of the sultan's reserve corps. The girls remain with their mothers until they are old enough to be chosen for the harem.

Until the last twenty years there were no common schools in Turkey for the children. Girls grew up to know nothing beyond what they heard and saw while with their mothers.

The Bosphorus is a channel eighteen miles long, connecting the sea of Marmora with the Black sea. The heights on both sides are very picturesque. The villages and large towns along the shore are built upon terraced plateaus extending up the heights. The Turks prefer the buildings nearest the water; the foreigners are obliged to occupy the terraces.

Conspicuous among the buildings along the shores are the

palace, the mosques or houses of worship with their gilded domes and minarets, and the kiosks, or summer houses. Not the least conspicuous nor the least important building one sees on the Bosphorus is Robert College, situated on the heights called Romili Hissar. This college was established by Dr. Hamlin, an American missionary, who spent over forty years of his life in the Orient. Mr. Robert of New York city gave the money for the erection of the building, and partly endowed it.

This college is for the secular, scientific and the theological education of young men from the East. There are text-books in several different languages used in the college. But all the students must learn something of English during the course of study.

In the Turkish mosques but few women are seen ; the public service is generally attended only by men. Five times in the twenty-four hours the mosque officials must go to the top of the minarets and call out the hour for prayer. The women perform their religious devotions in their own apartments.

There are many steam ferry boats in constant service on the Bosphorus. These boats have an apartment curtained off on the stern deck for Turkish women, which is furnished with low stools about a foot high, where they enjoy their gossip and smoke their cigarettes.

The Turks have a peculiar system of their own for calculating the hour of the day. The clock dial has twenty-four divisions, including two zeros which take the place of the figure 12, and the figures 1, 2, 3, etc., up to 11, are repeated twice. They begin the reckoning of the twenty-four hours at sunset, which is marked zero, and when the indicator points to the figure 1 it is called one o'clock P. M., and likewise the hours are indicated until the pointer reaches the second zero, when one hour, or division, from that time is called one o'clock A. M. Consequently the indicator recording the time on clock and watch dials must be changed every day to agree with the moment of sunset. For example: If the sun sets at five o'clock P. M., meridian time, one hour from that time the pointer indicates one o'clock P. M., and so continues to mark the hours until the second zero is reached, and then the figure 1 indicates one o'clock A. M. By the meridian reckoning of time we call one hour after midday one o'clock P. M., one hour after midnight one o'clock A. M.

The Bosphorus steamers and ferry boats run by Turkish time, and until the foreigner learns to calculate the difference between meridian and local time in Constantinople he finds himself constantly embarrassed in regard to the running time of the boats, which are the principal means of travel from point to point along the shores of the Bosphorus.

Constantinople is a very old city. It was first called Byzantium, and after the Roman empire was divided into two parts it was the capital of the division called the Eastern empire. It received its present name from Constantine the Great. Naturally there are many most interesting objects to attract the visitor in this ancient capital. But we have much yet to see before we complete our journey, and must therefore leave the beautiful shores of the Bosphorus for a yet older country, the land of Egypt.

CHAT VI.

IN EGYPT.

The World's Seven Wonders—The Ruins of the Brazen Colossus—Cleopatra's Needles—Cicero's Novel Sights—Palaces that are Marvels of Luxury and Beauty—The Pyramids—Huge Cheops—Higher than the Highest Dome or Spire—How the Khedive took in his Brother's Family of Five Hundred—The Story with which a Sheik Entertained a Prince—The Lady Badoura and the Jealous Emir—The Happy Ending of a Woful Seperation—How a Cairo Merchant Sells Goods—The Rajah who Wooed and Won a Donkey Driver's Daughter—How a Little Black-Eyed Teacher Became a Princess—The Gift of the Nile—Grain Fields for Deserts—Teaching Little Mohammedans—Dancing and Howling Dervishes—Places that Tradition Connects with the Infancy of Moses and Jesus—The Crossing of the Red Sea.

On leaving the shores of the Bosphorus and sailing through our steamer passed the Dardanelles, island after island, famous in Grecian legend and history. We touched at the island of Rhodes, where once stood the Colossus which was one of the seven wonders of the world. The visible portion of this monument ages since disappeared, but the foundations still remain deeply imbedded in the sands of the sea. It is said that the ruins of the Colossus were sold to a Jewish merchant who carried off seven hundred camel-loads of the metal. The brass of this statue 880 years after its fall amounted to 720,000 pounds.

It was taken to a European city, sold for a large amount of money and recast into various monuments.

The other six wonders of the world were the Pyramids of Egypt, the Hanging Gardens of Babylon, the tomb of Mausolus, king of Caria, the temple of Diana at Ephesus, the statue of Jupiter at Olympia by Phidas, made of ivory and gold, and the palace of Syrus, cemented with gold.

The Pyramids of Egypt, which may yet endure for ages to come, are all that is left of these marvelous structures.

We enter Egypt at Alexandria, which is an important commercial port on the Mediterranean coast, and the sea port of Cairo. There is not much of interest for the general tourist in Alexandria. The companion obelisk to the Egyptian column now standing in Central park, New York city, still remains on its "native heath," lying in a horizontal position, partly imbedded in the sand. I have had the pleasure of seeing these two obelisks—called Cleopatra's Needles—in their original bed in Alexandria, where they had been lying side by side for ages. At that time the question was, how could the obelisk now in America be taken to that country, for it is of very great weight and bulk. But such a gift was not to be declined, and the "ways and means" were soon found by which to transport this remarkable work of antiquity to our country.

Egypt is called the land of the Pharaohs. Cairo is its principal city. The streets of Cairo are full of novel sights; the natives go about on donkeys and camels; the women are closely veiled when they are in the streets. Some fine Arabian horses are seen, which are in the service of the official and domestic households of the khedive or sovereign, whose family and retainers number many hundreds.

The favorite ladies of the khedive's harem, as the feminine portion of his household is called, go closely veiled about the city in magnificent equipages; they make rounds of visits from palace to palace of the khedive's various households, with nothing to do but to admire each other's fine dress and beautiful jewels, and to gossip about the details of harem life. The palaces are marvels of luxury and beauty. The khedive's new palace, when finished, will be perhaps the largest and most magnificent in existence. Egypt is the home of the Oriental alabaster, and much of the beautiful stone enters into the construction of this palace. The grounds are enclosed by miles of stone wall ten feet high, and have a frontage on the river Nile of three and a half miles. There is a group of three palaces within the walls, connected by corridors already finished. and others are building.

There is so much generally known about the Pyramids of Egypt that I will only give dimensions of the largest one in the group called the Pyramid of Cheops. It is four hundred and eighty feet high; each of the four sides measures seven hundred and sixty feet at the base on the ground level. Its height, measured from the surface of the ground, exceeds the highest towers and steeples in Europe, and yet much of the original base is imbedded in the sand. To the top of the tower of the Strasburg cathedral from the ground measures four hundred and sixty-one feet; St. Peter's at Rome lifts its cross-crowned dome to the height of four hundred and thirty-seven feet; St. Paul's in London measures from the ground to the pinnacle on the dome three hundred and sixty-five feet.

Several years ago a brother of the khedive, residing in Constantinople, died; he left a family of five hundred persons, all told, to be cared for. The khedive ordered two small steamers to go to Constantinople and bring the family to Alexandria, where a beautiful palace was assigned to their service.

I was invited to pay a visit to the princess Monsoor, a daughter of the khedive's favorite wife. Harem life in Cairo is in general detail the same as in Constantinople. The routine of daily life among the women consists in visiting, smoking pipes and cigarettes and coffee drinking. Princess Mansoor is a beautiful blonde Circassian ; she was attired in a rich brown silk dress with trimmings of tortoise shell, upon the face of which was wrought a crescent and the letter I, the letter standing for Ishmail, the name of the reigning khedive at that time.

In regard to the name of Mansoor, the following story was told me. The tale was originally related by Ibn Mansoor, a sheik of olden times, and one of the high caliph's boon companions.

One of the Arabian princess, called the Prince of the Faithful, had many cares on his mind, and one night he became very restless and could not sleep. He summoned one of his retainers, Mesrour by name, and ordered him to bring some one to his chamber to divert him. Mesrour replied, "O my lord prince, will you not come out into the palace garden and amuse yourself with looking at the flowers, and observe the planets, and see the beautiful moon seated upon her throne of silver stars?" The prince answered, "O Mesrour, verily my soul wishes for nothing of that kind." "O my lord, most high and noble," rejoined Mesrour, "then order the learned men and poets to come before thee, that they may enter into discussions, and recite verses to thee, or relate wonderful tales to thine ear." The prince again replied that neither did his soul incline to any such amusement. "O my lord," continued Mesrour, "order the pages and the boon companions, and the men of polite manners, to come before thee to give an entertainment of witticisms and pleasant speech."

At this suggestion the prince was well pleased, and said, "O Mesrour, see who of the boon companions may be without the door." The bidding was obeyed, and Mesrour quickly returned, saying, "O my lord, Ali, Ibn Mansoor, the wag of

Damascus, is at the door." The prince ordered that he should enter the chamber at once.

Ibn Mansoor came into the presence of the prince and said, after making his salaam, "Peace be on thee, O Prince of the Faithful." The prince returned the salutation and spoke, "O Ibn Mansoor, may it please you to relate to us a story." "O Prince of the Faithful," replied Mansoor, "shall I relate a thing that I have witnessed, or a thing whereof I have heard?" The prince answered, "If you have seen anything extraordinary relate it to us." "Then," said Mansoor, "O Prince of the Faithful, give me thy hearing and thy mind." To which the prince replied, "O Ibn Mansoor, I hear with mine ears, I see with mine eyes, and I attend with my mind."

Then continued Mansoor and said, "O Prince of the Faithful, know that I have an appointment every year with Mohammed, the son of Hashimi, the Sultan of Balsora. I went to him as I was wont, and found him ready for the chase. He saluted me according to his custom, and bade me to mount and accompany him to the chase. But I replied, 'O my lord Sultan, I have not the power to ride, therefore I beg thee to seat me in the mansion and give charge to the chamberlain respecting me, and I will await thy return.'

"The Sultan did as I suggested, and then went his way to the chase. I was well treated, and entertained sumptuously. After a time I said to myself, 'By Allah! it is wonderful that I know so little of Balsora and I have been coming here many years. I only know the way from the palace to the garden, and from the garden to the palace. When shall I find a better opportunity to amuse myself with a view of the quarters?' And so I arose and walked out into the outer garden. Now thou knowest, O Prince of the Faithful, that there are in Balsora seventy streets, the length of each being three leagues.

"In the course of my wanderings I lost my way in its

by-streets, and being overcome with thirst I went to a great door near at hand which had upon it two large rings of brass, and a curtain of red hung over it. I stopped to divert myself with a view of the mansion, and while standing there I heard a voice of lamentation warbling melodious sounds.

"I approached the door and slightly raised the curtain: and lo! I beheld a fair damsel. While looking at her she chanced to cast a glance toward the door and saw me standing there with the curtain half raised. She ordered one of the slave-girls to inquire who was at the door. The girl advanced and said, 'O sheik, have you no modesty? What right have you to enter a harem that is not your own?' I answered, saying, 'O mistress, I have a good excuse for doing so. It is this: I am a stranger in Balsora and have lost my way, and am suffering greatly with a dreadful thirst from which I have almost perished.

"The damsel called another slave attendant and said, 'O Lutf, give to the stranger at the door a draught of water in the mug of gold.' Straightway a mug of shining gold set with jewels, and filled with perfumed water, covered with a napkin of green silk, was brought and handed to me. I prolonged my drinking, O Prince of the Faithful, stealing glances the while at the beautiful maiden. Whereupon the damsel said, 'O sheik, go your way.' 'O my beautiful mistress,' said I, 'I am greatly troubled in mind.' 'Respecting what?' inquired the damsel. 'I am thinking,' said I, 'of the former owner of this beautiful mansion, who was a sincere friend of mine in his life-time. He had great riches: has he left any children?' 'Yes,' said the maiden, 'he has left a daughter called Badoura, and she has inherited all his treasures.' 'Then,' said I, 'O my sweet mistress, are you the daughter?' 'Yes, O sheik. You have prolonged your discourse, now go your way.'

"'Yes, I must go,' replied I, 'that I know. But I see you

are sad, and disturbed in mind. Perhaps God may grant you relief by means of me.' To which she replied, 'O sheik, if you are indeed of the number of those who are worthy of being intrusted with secrets, then will I reveal mine. Inform me who you may be.'

"I told her my name, and that I was one of the boon companions of the High Caliph in Damascus. When she heard my name spoken, O Prince of the Faithful, she saluted me and said, 'Welcome, thrice welcome, O Ibn Mansoor, I will acquaint you with my secret. I am a separated and a disconsolate lover. I love Jubir, the Emir of the tribe of Sheiban.' I asked, 'What, O mistress of the beautiful, is the cause of this unhappy separation?' 'The cause was this, and this only,' mournfully answered the damsel. 'One day I was sitting on a mat by the open door. Ubysino, my slave girl, was combing my hair, and when she had finished with the work, she inclined her face to my head and kissed my braided tresses. Just at that moment Jubir, the noble, passed by the door, and seeing the act of love of my slave, he determined straightway upon a separation, and recited this verse :—

If another have a share in the object of my love,
I abandon my beloved, and live alone forever.

And since that unlucky day, O sheik, have I heard no word from him.'

"'And what do you desire of me, O mistress Badoura?' She replied, 'O sheik, I desire to send him a letter by you. If you bring me answer from Jubir, I will give you five hundred pieces of gold. If you bring no answer, I will give you one hundred pieces of gold as compensation for the long walk.'

"The fair damsel, O high prince, quickly wrote the letter and gave it to me.

"I went to the palace of Jubir; he was not at home. After a time, lo! he appeared, mounted upon a steed caparisoned with jewels and fine cloth. When he observed me, he saluted and embraced me. We went into the house and he ordered the table to be brought laden with choice viands. The table was made of precious woods; the feet were of gold, and upon it were many kinds of savory food. Then Jubir said, 'Let us stretch forth our hands and comfort our hearts by eating of this provision.' 'But,' I replied, 'by Allah, O Jubir, I will not eat of your food until you have satisfied my desire.' Whereupon Jubir asked, 'What then, O sheik, is your desire?'

"I handed him the letter from Badoura, which he read and tore into a thousand pieces, and gave the bits of paper to the wind, saying, 'O Ibn Mansoor, whatsoever you desire except—be it understood—an answer to this letter, you can have. To this letter I have no reply to give.'

"Straightway, O Prince of the Faithful, Jubir fell into a fit and was carried to his chamber. After a time, a slave-woman came to me with a bag of gold, as much as I was able to carry in one hand, and said, 'O sheik, my master sends this to you. Now go your way.'

"I returned to the damsel with the sorrowful tidings that I came without answer to her letter. Then she said mournfully, 'O Ibn Mansoor, night and day succeed not one another during the course of an event without changing it.' Then she raised her eyes towards heaven, O great prince, and said: 'O object of my worship, my Master and my Lord, as Thou hast afflicted me by the love of Jubir, so do Thou afflict him by the love of me.' Then she gave me the promised hundred pieces of gold, and I went immediately to the sultan of Balsora. He also paid me a sum of gold, and I returned to Bagdad.

"When the next year arrived, O Prince of the Faithful, I repaired again to Balsora and performed my service to the sultan, for which I received my full compensation. I then bethought myself, O prince, of the damsel, Badoura, and I said to myself, 'by Allah, I must go and seek information concerning her.' Forthwith I went to the mansion and found the ground before her door had been swept and sprinkled, and many servants were there. I believed the damsel had died of her great grief, and that one of the emirs had taken up his abode in her dwelling. Sadly I turned away without making inquiry about the maiden, and went to the house of Jubir. Then I found the marble benches in front of the door demolished; there were no pages standing near, and I stood and bewailed in mournful verse the sad fate of these two people.

"Soon came out a slave-girl and said, 'O sheik, be silent; may you be bereft of your mother! Wherefore bewail you so before this door?' I answered, 'This mansion was once the home of a good friend of mine, and now he is no more.' The servant replied, 'It is not even so. Jubir is still blest with his riches, but God has afflicted him with the love of a beautiful damsel named Lady Badoura, and he is so overwhelmed by his love for her that he is like a great overthrown rock; he neither eats, nor drinks, nor sleeps.' 'Go ask permission,' said I, 'of your master to let me come to his chamber.'

"I found the unhappy man, O Prince of the Faithful, like a mass of stone thrown down, understanding neither sign nor speech. The servant said to me, 'O sheik, if you know any consoling verses, recite them to my master.' Accordingly I repeated to Jubir a very pathetic love ditty, which pleased him greatly, O most excellent prince.'

"He opened his eyes and said to me, 'Welcome, welcome, O Ibn Mansoor. Will you go straightway and take a letter to her I love?'

"It was quickly written, and read as follows: 'I conjure you by Allah, O my well beloved mistress, act gently towards me; love hath deprived me of my reason. My passion for you hath enslaved me, and clad me with garments of sickness, and rendered me pitiable. I was wont before this to think lightly of love, and to regard it, O my beloved mistress, as an easy matter. But when it had shown me the waves of its sea, I submitted to God's judgment. If you will, O my mistress, have mercy, and grant me a meeting; and if you will, kill me; but still forget not to show mercy and favor.'

"I stood again before her door: all was quiet. I gently raised the curtain, and lo, I saw ten slave-girls as beautiful as the stars seated upon low cushions, with the princess Badoura in their midst, shining in her beauty like the full moon. O, Prince of the Faithful, happily she observed me, and welcomed me kindly.

"I gave to her the letter; she read its contents and was well pleased. Said she, 'O Ibn Mansoor, I will send by you my answer.' She wrote once, twice and thrice, and tore the paper in pieces each time. Again she wrote, and this time, O Prince of the Good, she sealed the words and bid me carry them on the wings of the wind. I said, 'No, O Mistress of the Moon, I cannot take a message whose contents I know not of.' She then recited her letter, which read as follows:

"'How long, O how long, shall this coyness and aversion continue, O Jubir, my beloved? Perhaps I did commit a wrong, and if so, I was not aware of it. Then inform me wherefore hast thou done this. I did desire to welcome thee, O Jubir, the noble, as I welcome sleep to my eyelids. And since thou, too, hast drank of the pure cup of love, welcome, thrice welcome, O Jubir, star of my heaven.'

"I said, 'Well done, good and virtuous damsel; now I will carry the message.'

"I took the letter, O prince, and gave it into the hands of Jubir. He opened and read, and then said, 'O Ibn Mansoor, did she write this with her hands?' I replied, 'By Allah, she did; do people write with their feet?' And O Prince of the

Best, my words were not yet ended when we heard the clinking of her anklets in the corridor. On beholding her whom he loved, Jubir arose upon his feet. The pain of his heart and the heaviness of his limbs had left him.

"Jubir seated himself again, and said to Badoura, 'Wherefore, O my beloved mistress, hast thou not sat down?' She answered, turning her beaming eyes upon me, and said, 'O sheik, I will sit me down only upon one condition;' and, O Prince, she bent her beautiful head over to me and whispered some secret words, whereupon I sent a slave to do my bidding, and soon came a cadi* and two witnesses.

"Jubir then arose and gave the cadi a purse containing a thousand pieces of gold, and said, 'O cadi, perform the ceremony of marriage between this damsel and me.' It was done, O Prince of the Faithful, and I went my way rejoicing. But, O Prince, I have yet whereof to tell you. As I was lifting the curtain to go out, the Princess Badoura called me back and put into my hands a purse containing three thousand pieces of gold. What think ye of that, O prince?"

By this time the restlessness of the Prince of the Faithful had ceased, and his heart had dilated. He said, "O Ibn Monsoor, go forth and bring to me a damsel as fair and as good as the Princess Badoura, and three thousand pieces of gold are thine."

There are miles of bazars in Cairo; they occupy a large tract of land in the heart of the city. Here may be seen products from every part of the East, even from the Indies. The bazaars are small booths not more than ten feet square. The merchant sits cross-legged, Turkish fashion, upon a low table in the center of his little shop, with his pipe in his mouth. The goods for sale are heaped together on shelves within hand's reach of the master of the shop. He does not importune cus-

* A doctor of the Law.

tomers to buy, but rather, the customer must ask him as a favor to show the goods, which is done by the merchant's pointing to a pile of rich stuffs heaped up in the corner: but if the pile is beyond the master's reach, he will ask the customer to hand the pile to him! Apparently he is indifferent about making a sale, but if the customer turns to leave the shop without purchasing, then the merchant assumes quite another manner. He is upon his feet in a moment, and is all smiles and affability. Gold and silver ornaments and jewelry are sold by weight at a fixed price for the metal, and an additional small sum is asked for the workmanship. The gold and silver are warranted by the merchant to be pure metal.

I visited the American Mission School in Cairo for Arab and Egyptian girls. There I heard a very remarkable story of one of the little school-girls, which occurred only a few years before. The story was told me by the mistress of the school, and was as follows: A certain East Indian rajah many years ago abandoned the religious faith of his people and accepted the Christian belief. He went to England, where he purchased a beautiful property, including a palace, and lived in grand style. The prince was very rich, and a kind-hearted man withal. He freely bestowed good gifts upon the poor. The rajah was received kindly by the royal family.

On a certain occasion the rajah passed through Cairo on his way for a visit to the home of his ancestors in India. He had heard of this Mission School, and being interested in the work of Christian education, he called upon the lady director of the school, without giving his name or rank, and made known his desire to visit the classes. He was invited into one of the class rooms, where were sixteen young Egyptian girls, barefooted and scantily clad, seated on the floor receiving instruction from one a little older than themselves, who sat within the circle. The rajah was at once captivated by the earnest manner and the large and expressive black eyes of the young teacher, who kept her position on the floor, and looked unhappy that her class had been disturbed.

After leaving the room the rajah made some inquiries regarding the young teacher, and said to the directress of the school that he would like to make that young girl his wife; the lady was not agreeably impressed by the suggestion, from one who was an entire stranger. She told him that she had reclaimed the girl from a very low life; that she had been a donkey-driver; that she had found her living with her mother in a little donkey-stable, and being a bright little girl she had permission of the mother to take her into the school, saying that she was now educated to a point where she was useful as an assistant in the school, and therefore begged the unknown suitor to make no further allusion to the subject. The rajah thanked the lady for her kindness, and asked permission to return the next day.

On the following day, at the appointed hour, the rajah came again and presented his card, with an autograph letter from Queen Victoria. The rajah wished to visit the school again, and on his departure renewed his request to be permitted to make the young Egyptian teacher his wife, giving as his reason for his sudden falling in love, that the girl's eyes and earnest manner had completely captivated him. He said he would place her under proper tuition and training immediately after marriage, in order to fit her for a position of usefulness which she could never otherwise obtain. He desired the directress of the school to communicate his proposition to the girl, to whom he had not yet addressed one word, and said he would call on the following day for her decision. Accordingly the wishes of the rajah were made known to the girl.

The simple-minded girl, not yet fifteen years old, did not understand one word what was meant by marriage, and entreated her kind guardian not to send her into slavery. She wept bitterly at the thought of being sent away, and was only pacified when told that she should not go unless entirely willing to do so after she fully understoood what the proposal meant.

The rajah came again on the third day, and showed papers which fully satisfied the principal of the school that his motives were pure and noble. He then desired to speak with the girl, which was done in the presence of the lady. He addressed the girl in the Arabic language, which was understood by the teacher. The interview greatly terrified the timid creature, and, with tears in her eyes, she again implored her foster-mother not to send her away into slavery.

The rajah went away not discouraged in his suit. He made the request that the girl should have a place in the family, and be taught European manners, and that she should be suitably dressed at his expense. Until this time she had never sat at a table to eat, but had taken her food sitting on the floor or under a tree in the garden. The rajah informed the lady that he should return to England in a few months, and on his way he would stop in Cairo, when he hoped to be able to win the girl for his wife, if at that time no objections should be raised.

The rajah's wishes were carried out with the most satisfactory results. The young girl began to understand her future destiny, and was willing to acquire the education planned for her, although she continually regretted the day the rajah first saw her.

The rajah, as arranged, in due time gave information of his return from India, and requested that suitable clothing should be provided for the girl if she were willing to become his wife. He came at the promised time, and the girl was now willing to accept him as her husband. Her father, an European, living in Alexandria, was found, and informed that his presence was desired that he might give his unknown daughter in marriage. The mother, a poor Egyptian donkey-driver, living in a mud hovel, was entirely ignorant of what was in store for her child.

The marriage was celebrated in the mission house, upon which occasion the rajah gave the directress £1,000 sterling, to invest in such a way as she might deem advisable to advance the Christian education of the poor children in Cairo. Upon every anniversary of the wedding day, which occurred many years ago, the sum of £1,000 has been received for the mission work. With this large yearly donation, a residence, a church, and a school-house have been built for the American Mission in Cairo.

The rajah was true to his word. He placed his wife in a separate apartment in his palace and provided her with teachers. At the end of two years she was presented at Court, and from that time forward a new life was opened to her. She received the title of princess, and shared her husband's position in society, and became what she most desired to be, a benefactor of the poor and wretched.

The valley of the river Nile is made very productive by the yearly inundations which occur at certain seasons of the year, leaving a deposit of rich alluvial soil, thus changing the desert land for miles back from the river shores into rich grain fields. By irrigation the sandy soil of Cairo is transposed into beautiful gardens and made to blossom and bear fruit luxuriantly. Herodotus called Egypt "the gift of the Nile," because the country owes its productiveness to the overflowing of the river, without which the entire country would be a desert. In ancient times the long valley of the Nile was called the granary of Rome.

There are about four hundred mosques or Mohammedan houses of worship in Cairo, and every mosque has a school attached, where, if nothing more is taught, the children are at least instructed in the principles of their religion. As soon as a Mohammedan child can talk it is taught to recite, "I testify that there is no deity but God, and I testify that Mohammed is his prophet." They must also recite daily portions from the Koran. The weekly sum of three cents is paid for school tuition.

The dervishes of Cairo are a very unprepossessing people to look at. They have two religious orders: one is called the howling and the other the dancing dervishes. They may have families, but must spend two nights a week in their convents. Their religion consists mainly in mortifying the flesh, repeating prayers and performing exercises in dancing and howling. They observe a weekly fast of twelve hours, and hold meetings twice a week for dancing and howling. There are no women in these orders. By a backsheesh, or gift, I obtained admission to one of their religious meetings. Thirty men took part in it. They began by dancing in a semi-circle in front of the sheik, or chief, and having made salaams, they moved backward and forward in a circle around the sheik, kneeling on blankets. After having bowed their heads repeatedly to the floor, they began their devotions by making incomprehensible movements with the arms, accompanied by horrid tones from several discordant musical instruments. Rising, they again bowed their heads low, and then began a rapid dancing movement performed in a circle around the sheik, all moving together in unison and in time with the music. As the music increased in rapidity and became louder, the devotees increased the violence of their movements, until their disheveled hair made them still more hideous, and their vociferations were intensified to an almost deafening degree. After a time they began whirling, their bodies spinning around like tops; the faster the music the quicker their motions and the more piercing their shrieks became. Suddenly at the beat of a drum the circle of whirling fanatics broke, and again advancing in a semi-circle before the sheik, they repeated their salutations, put on the dirty robes they had cast off at the commencement of the ceremony and fell down on the floor exhausted.

According to tradition Cairo is a very interesting landmark in biblical history. We read that on a certain occasion Pharaoh's daughter went down to the river to take a bath, and there found a young child hidden in the deep grass on the river bank, and that she took the infant to herself and named him Moses, meaning drawn out of the water. A little thicket of bulrushes just on the shore of the Nile, in the heart of the town, is said to have been the very spot where the infant Moses was concealed by his mother from the executioner of Pharaoh, King of Egypt.

At Heliopolis, now a wretched Arabian town of mud houses about an hour's drive from Cairo, is the old sycamore tree under which it is said Joseph and Mary, with the infant Jesus, rested during their flight into Egypt. This tradition renders the tree an object of great interest to the Christian tourist, who often performs his devotions there. It is called the "Virgin's Tree." Its trunk near the base is about ten feet in diameter, and its wide-spreading branches shade a large area of ground. It is enclosed by a high fence, else there would not be left a branch of this tree by the insatiable memento-collecting tourist, who would have carried it all away long before this.

Near Suez, a few hours' distance from Cairo, is the head of the Red Sea, where the children of Israel crossed over when they were pursued by the Egyptians. We read in the Bible that the waters parted, rolled up on both sides like walls, and the Israelites crossed over on dry land; but when their pursuers came upon the opposite bank and entered upon the dry path, the waters immediately came together and they were swallowed up in the deep. It is a fact that at times at this point, from the operation of the tides and winds, the waters do actually recede so as to leave almost a pathway across the sea. There is a ship canal now through the Isthmus of Suez, by which vessels, plying between Europe and the East Indies, pass from the Mediterranean to the Red Sea It was made under the direction of the famous civil engineer, Count de Lesseps.

CHAT VII.

ARABIA AND INDIA.

Sailing Down the Red Sea—Mount Sinai and the Arabians—Mohammed—The Divers—Jugglers and Snake-Charmers—Ostrich Droves—Into the Indian Ocean—The Cruelty of an African King—The Tower of Silence—Sun Worshipers—Burning the Body of his Wife—Thrown into the Ganges—The Riches of an Indian Jungle—The Homes of Calcutta—The Awful Fate of Hindoo Widows—A Tree that Shades more than Two Acres—Chaste—A Visit from the Rajah—His Present of Flowers and Fish and Taffy Candy—Riding on an Elephant—Wreaths of Yellow Flowers in the Sacred River—A Million Years for a Hair—The Most Beautiful Structure in Existence—Walls of Precious Stones—Roses of Coral and Lilies of Mother-of-Pearl—Diamonds and Rubies—The Boy from the Wolf's Den—Cashmere Shawls—The Peacock Throne—The Shah's Jeweled Turban.

In my journey from Egypt to India I passed Mount Sinai, which is near Suez, where we stopped at the end of our last evening's chat. Mount Sinai is a very interesting landmark in biblical history; the ten commandments were inscribed on two tablets of stone and given to Moses by the Lord. The mountain is a bare, rocky peak rising from the desert. There is a monastery on the side of the mountain, where travelers are entertained by the monks. But few people are seen there besides the wandering tribes of Arabs. The ancient Arabians were a superstitious race; their favorite study was the interpretation of dreams. They were very hospitable; in the region of Mount Sinai they always kept the "fires of hospitality" blazing at night, so that the weary pilgrims going to Mecca, the sacred city of the Mohammedans, could find a place of rest. They were as cruel in their revenge as they were generous in their hospitality. A willful offence was never forgiven.

Mecca, which is far to the south of Mount Sinai, is a sacred city to the Mohammedans, because it was the birth-place of Mohammed. Mohammed was of obscure birth and a camel driver, but he rose to be a great spiritual guide, simply by his honesty of purpose, the unselfishness of his daily life, and his constant devotion to the religious creed which he taught. He did not pretend to introduce a new religion; he wished to restore the true primitive faith as it existed in the days of the patriarchs and prophets of the early times, as his people had fallen into the gross worship of idols. After he reached the years of manhood he retired once a year to a cave near Mecca, where he devoted himself for one month to fasting, prayer and meditation. The great ambition of Mohammedans is to make a pilgrimage to Mecca, and pray at the tomb of their prophet which is there. All who have accomplished this devotional journey are called Hadjis; and all who are descended from Mohammed wear a green turban, a color which they consider sacred.

From Mount Sinai I sailed down the Red Sea, along the shores of Arabia. I saw many coffee plantations on the mountain slopes on the coast of the Red Sea, with here and there the mud huts of the natives, and swarms of naked children gamboling about in their sports near the shore. From the deck of our English steamer, when lying at anchor in the bay of Aden, I saw a dozen or more men and boys diving in the water for pennies and sixpences thrown from the deck of the vessel; they also made many curious evolutions in the water, appar-

SNAKE CHARMERS IN BENARES, INDIA.

ently as much at home there as are the fish. These divers would climb to the top of the ship's masts and, leaping into the water with a wooden ball in each hand, would come to the surface with the coin held between the teeth.

I saw also at that time the jugglers and snake-charmers performing on the deck of the ship. They brought their snakes on board in bags, letting them out of the bags. The snake-charmers seemed to have perfect control over the reptiles by means of music from a rude wind instrument. When the performance was finished they put the snakes again into the bags, which were then snugly tied up. These magicians swarm on the decks of passenger vessels while at anchor in these seas. One of the most wonderful feats is to produce small pots of growing plants from their long, flowing sleeves, although they bare their arms to show the bystanders that they do not have the pots in their sleeves. If these impromptu showmen pick up a few sixpences they leave the ship jubilant over their success.

And I saw many droves of ostriches, black, white and gray in color, roving around at will; the vicinity of Aden is famous for ostrich farming; the natives bring on board the passenger steamers bags of beautiful ostrich plumes and sell them at very moderate prices.

As we proceeded on our voyage I caught glimpses of the coasts of Abyssinia and Nubia, and of the picturesque scenery on both sides of the narrow and rocky channel forming the entrance from the Red Sea to the Indian Ocean, called by the natives the Straits of Bab-el-Mandeb, but named by the English sailors "The Gate of Lamentation," because of the many accidents and shipwrecks which have happened there. I began now to realize that I was indeed far away from home, for the diversified prospect presented quite a different appearance to anything I had seen before. But on and on we sailed, reflecting the while on the vast difference between this eastern land and our own country, and the incomparable situation of the two peoples.

Arabia and Africa are parts of the world but little known by Americans from actual observation. They have not much attraction for the pleasure tourist. In fact, I think the curious traveler would find an unwelcome reception in some portions of these lands. There are constant dissensions among the tribes in the interior of Africa, and their warfare is carried on most barbarously.

I have heard it related that in one of the African districts remote from the sea-coast occurs what might be called the annual anniversary of human sacrifice. It is the occasion when the king of a certain tribe chooses a wife, which he does once a year. A dozen of the finest of their maidens are selected and attired with feathers and ornamented with bright colors painted on the skin. After the customary hideous ceremony has been performed, which passes for a solemnity among these barbarians, these young girls are filed in review before the king, who is mounted on a horse, and from their number he chooses one for a wife, who is set up on the horse behind him. In the meantime, if any one of his wives become disagreeable to him, she is conducted into the column of the remaining eleven. At a signal the girls start upon a run for dear life in all directions, the mounted king chasing down all these poor creatures, trampling upon them and killing such as may fall by the way. If any succeed in making their escape in this terrible race, they are killed in solemn sacrifice. This horrible custom was begun generations ago by a very cruel king who wished to make of his people a tribe of warriors, and availed himself of his supreme right over the lives of his subjects in order to lessen the number of women in his tribe.

Our steamer arrived at the city of Bombay in India after an agreeable tropical voyage across the Indian ocean. I saw

AN INDIAN CARRIAGE AND PAIR, BOMBAY.

in Bombay the Tower of Silence, the Parsees' burial place for the dead. It is a high, square built tower, open at the top, and has a small door at the base. In the place of a floor is an iron grating, and the vultures fly down from the top of the tower and take off the flesh from the bones, which when bared fall between the bars into a pit of quick-lime.

The Parsees are descended from the ancient Persians. They are very earnest in their religious devotions. They worship the sun, not only as the life-giving source of light and heat, but as a symbol of divinity. They kneel down wherever they chance to be at the hour of sunset and perform their devotions with their faces turned toward the west. They have no temples or houses of worship. They live together in large families, or groups of relations; often as many as fifty persons live in one house. The Parsees in Bombay are a picturesque-looking people. They wear high sugar-loaf shaped hats, of black felt, wide flowing pantaloons of yellow or blue silk, a long frock tunic of another colored silk, confined at the waist by a silken girdle or a chain of gold or silver, and an aigrette of precious stones on the left breast. The little boys are dressed exactly like their fathers. Parsee women are not seen in the streets; they are strictly domestic, rarely leaving their houses. The Parsees are fond of traveling and go about the world considerably. They are a prosperous people; in Bombay they are chiefly merchants and do most of the banking business.

I found in my travels a great difference in the methods of disposing of the dead among the nations. The Hindoos burn the dead on funeral pyres. Cremation is performed by the Hindoos in an open court; the mourners prepare the pile of wood upon which to lay the body; after applying the torch they wait to see the body consumed to ashes, and then move sorrowfully away.

The following account of the burning of a dead person in Calcutta was related to me by one who was present on that occasion. The remains of a woman were brought to the court on a board by two coolies, or laborers; the husband of the deceased began at once to bargain for the wood wanted for the pyre. When the necessary amount was secured it was piled up to the height of about four feet on the stone flagging in the yard. The body, covered with a piece of coarse canvas, was then laid upon the pile of wood; the husband partly uncovered it and removed the rings, anklets and bangles, and then anointed the body with grease. Some fine-cut wood was laid over it by a coolie, after which a Hindoo priest advanced, and the bereaved man threw a half-dozen copper pieces at his feet. The priest demanded more, and three more pieces were given, which were all the man had. Then a small basin containing rice and millet-seed mixed with goats' milk was brought and handed to the husband, together with two small sticks of sandal-wood. The priest blessed these articles, and the husband placed the sticks at the sides of the face of the dead woman, and put some of the mixture into the mouth and upon the neck. He then took a lighted fagot from the priest and went three times around the pyre, swinging the flaming fagot three times on each round, after which he set fire to the wood, and soon the pile was brightly blazing. The mourning Hindoo did not leave the ground until the last spark of fire had disappeared; he then turned sadly away, but he was not permitted to leave the ground until he had remunerated the coolie who had assisted; this he was not able to do until my informant gave him a few coppers, which enabled him to satisfy the demands of the coolie.

Among the better classes of the Hindoos, the ashes of the dead, together with the ashes of the consumed wood, are gathered up and thrown into the Ganges river, when it is possible

THE BURNING GHAT ON THE GANGES, AT BENARES.

to do so. The waters of the Ganges and also the waters of its various branches are considered sacred.

The Hindoos and Parsees are distinct peoples in appearance and customs, and totally different in their mode of life.

From Bombay to Calcutta by rail is about five days' journey. There is an immense tract of territory between these two cities which as yet has been scarcely trodden by man. It is inhabited only by birds, beasts and reptiles. Judging from the borders of this impenetrable jungle which I have seen, there must be within it untold treasures of beautiful woods, and an almost endless variety of tropical flora and fruits. This unknown territory is an inheritance for future generations, when its mysteries must be revealed and it must yield up its products as the demand for them increases.

Among the Hindoos the rajahs or governors of provinces dress very richly. They dress in velvets of all colors, embroidered with seed pearls; often precious stones are wrought in their garments, and they wear the red fez or cap decorated with aigrettes of feathers and jewels. The merchant class wear cashmere shawls, of a quality according to their rank and riches, thrown over the shoulders and waist, leaving the right arm bare, and long white cloth pantaloons, and a white cotton scarf twisted around the head. The Hindoo women seldom appear on foot in the streets of the large cities; they go about in palanquins, or palkas, as they are called by the foreigners. The palka is a long box, one side of which can be let down, with windows upon both sides, ; it contains a cushion and a pillow. The person takes a recumbent position; and when nicely packed away the side is closed up, and two coolies take up the conveyance with handles at each end and move along with a steady and measured tread. The occupant may read as he goes on his way, the movement of the palka being so steady there is scarcely a jar perceptible.

Calcutta is now within comparatively easy reach of the tourist in search of fresh objects to interest and entertain. It is not so many years ago, however, that a traveler was almost unknown in this far-off corner of the world. But the comfortable facilities offered by the steamships and railroads in the East at the present day, invite one to these distant wanderings. The more the globe is traversed the smaller it appears.

The facilities for travel by land and water have very greatly increased in the last twenty years, and according to the experience of the present age, the word of command for all is onward, onward.

A large portion of Calcutta is now like any other European city, having been built mostly by the English, who, as you know, rule India. In the native quarter the Hindoo home, with all its peculiar customs, is still seen. Entire families, including grandparents, parents and children, live in enclosures called compounds, each family having its own apartment. These compounds or homesteads pass from one generation to another. A compound or Indian mansion is a one-story building constructed around an open court, which has but one entrance from the street. The compound may be large or small, depending on the rank and wealth of the family. In an obscure corner of the building is an apartment assigned to the invalids among the women and children, who are not allowed to remain with those members of the family who are in health. What seems strange and inhuman to us is that the sick are attended only by servants, never by members of the family.

When the sons marry they bring their wives to the family compound, and occupy such apartment as the elder of the family—the father or eldest son—may assign to them. If the mother of the family is left a widow, she resigns her rank, her apartment and her jewels at once to the eldest married son, who bestows his mother's rank and possessions on his own

A HINDOO MOTHER AND CHILDREN.—GROUP OF INDIAN MEN AND WOMEN IN BOMBAY, INDIA.

wife. The mother then descends to the place of the lowest menial, really becoming of no account where she once lived almost as a sovereign, and becomes henceforth subject to the bidding of the family. However, if she is a woman of unusual intelligence she may sometimes be called in to give her advice on occasions of important family councils. It was because of her degradation that in former days the widow preferred to throw herself upon the funeral pyre of her husband and mingle her own ashes with his, rather than survive him and submit to the inevitable disgrace. But this horrible custom is a thing of the past in all localities where the English authority is felt, and without doubt in time it will entirely disappear.

One might ask how could it be possible that a woman in her sane mind, and of her own free will, could have the courage, or desperation, to throw herself upon a pile of burning wood? To us it seems incredible. But such was the custom among the Hindoos for many centuries. By request of the widow the nearest of kin, or the most affectionate one of the children, was chosen to assist her in the hour when she was to be subjected to this dreadful death. The woman, called the suttee, is made intoxicated by drinking the tea of a certain herb that has a powerfully intoxicating effect, and when she had become nearly senseless and scarcely able to stand, the person chosen for that purpose led her to the burning pyre and pushed her face downward upon it. Immediately she became suffocated and generally realized but little of the torture of burning to death.

The compound has its *zenana*, or women's quarters. The young girls live together, and entirely separate from the young boys. The wife serves the husband while he eats; now, following the European custom, he sits at a table, but the wife eats her meals sitting upon a mat on the floor, and never in the presence of her husband.

Among the Hindoos little girls are generally promised in

marriage at the age of eight to twelve years, sometimes even younger. As a recognition of this fact of her betrothal a small mark is made on the child's forehead with red paint, which is kept there until the girl is taken by the husband to his paternal compound. After the girl leaves her mother she seldom, or perhaps never, has the opportunity of meeting her family again.

The elder brother in a Hindoo family is not permitted to see the face of a younger brother's wife, but the younger brother may see and meet the elder brother's wife, as she is at any time liable to become the mistress of the household by the death of the mother. A cage life indeed is that of the Hindoo women.

The palace of the English viceroy, or Governor General of India, at Calcutta, is a noble building. Its appearance is not unlike that of the White House in Washington, but far more imposing. All the department buildings necessary to the office of the viceroy, together with a chapel, are within the same enclosure with the palace.

In the suburbs of Calcutta may be seen the largest banyan tree known to be in existence. Its main trunk has a circumference of more than fifty feet, and there are more than two hundred and twenty-five other stocks, which reach to the ground like smaller trunks, the most of them being good-sized trees; over two acres of ground are shaded by this patriarchal banyan.

The banyan is peculiar to India; it is the ordinary shade tree in the cities and smaller towns. As the stocks multiply too fast for the space, they are cut off. The banyan sends its shoots downward from the branches, which take root in the ground and become stocks of other trees; in this manner they spread over a large surface. As soon as a new shoot becomes rooted it sends out new branches near the parent branch where it started, and thus in time a small forest comes from one stock. I have heard that there was once a banyan on the Nerbuddah river, in the north of Hindostan, that had three hundred and

BANYAN TREE AT BARRACKPORE, NEAR CALCUTTA, INDIA.

fifty stocks, under whose shade seven thousand men could stand. The larger part of this tree was carried away by an inundation of the river.

From Calcutta we proceeded to Delhi, in the north of India. On the journey I tarried a little time at Benares, situated on the Ganges river. Here is the Mecca or great pilgrim resort of Hindostan and the home of the Brahmin priesthood. In Benares distinction in caste, or prescribed social rank, prevails more strictly, if possible, than elsewhere in Hindostan. There are four principal castes among the Hindoos; the highest is that of the Brahmins, who are born to the priesthood. A Hindoo would rather prefer the most menial service if it secured him the caste of the Brahmins, by which he could be privileged to wear the sacred white cord of their order over his right shoulder, than to belong to a lower caste with wealth at his command. They can eat only with those of their own caste. They must not even cook their food in vessels owned by persons of a lower caste, nor partake of food handled by them. Consequently they can never leave their own country. The Brahmins are regarded by the three other castes with profound veneration. They alone can officiate in the priesthood. Their high caste forbids them from following the ordinary ways of gaining a living; they generally depend upon alms for support. They may receive large gifts, in which case a blessing is granted the giver which is supposed to blot out every sin, and to assure a paradise upon earth. The different castes neither eat nor drink together, nor intermarry. They only associate in some great religious festivals. I have heard it said that there is a peculiar caste among the Hindoos holding itself so superior above all others that it will not permit its daughters to marry, because intermarriage is forbidden, and there is no caste high enough for them.

But the sons are permitted to wed women of another caste.

These distinctions of caste not only prevent the general elevation of the people, as may easily be supposed, but check the efforts made by others for their improvement.

Once so far away from home in our wanderings as to be in Benares, we thought it agreeable to prolong our stay and called to deliver a letter of introduction to Rajah Sambhee Narayana Sinhar, but he was not at home. An hour afterward he came in grand state to return the visit. He was dressed in blue silk trousers, a long pink silk frock, and yellow-toed slippers. On his fez was a cluster of precious stones. His servants, a half-dozen in number, were attired in gay colors, after the Eastern fashion. His coach was painted red, and was heavily gilded, and the trappings of the horses were gorgeous. The rajah speaks English fluently; he was educated at Queen's College in Benares. While speaking of the nobility of India, he said the rajahs often had from two to six hundred servants and retainers. It is said that most of these retainers serve without wages in the form of money, but they obtain rice and fish from their master's stores. They also receive many presents from visitors, and often a lodging as well. The rajah proposed to place at our service on the following day one of his elephants fully equipped and several of his servants to escort us through the city, and a boat that we might see some of the sights on the Ganges. Of course this offer was accepted with much pleasure.

Soon after the rajah's departure two of his servants returned, bringing baskets containing flowers, fruits, vegetables, an immense fish, a package of almonds, and a large cake of taffy candy made of brown sugar. Formerly it was the custom of the rajahs to give visitors bearing letters of introduction cashmere shawls; but unhappily for the guests this custom is falling out of use.

On the following day, according to promise, the rajah's elephant, one of a half-dozen, and fully as large as Barnum's

STATE ELEPHANTS OF THE VICEROY EQUIPPED FOR A JOURNEY, BENARES.

famous Jumbo, splendidly equipped with a howdah, or saddle, covered with red velvet and fringed with gold and spangles, made his appearance. This immense creature knelt down, and by means of a ladder we mounted to the howdah. Three servants took their places behind us and the driver seated himself astride the animal's neck. From time to time the elephant turned his head to look at us, as if he suspected that he was engaged in the unworthy service of carrying "Christian dogs," as we foreigners are called. However, he was not refractory, and readily obeyed the spear by which the mahout, or driver, guided him. Although horses and donkeys of India see elephants daily on the roads, they always show signs of fright when they come in their way. We made an excursion of four miles in this novel way. We met several naked dead bodies being carried to the crematory ground, followed by coolies bearing on their heads the wood for the fires.

Going along the Ganges I saw wreaths of yellow flowers floating on the water, which had been placed on the boxes containing the ashes of the dead who had been burned on the funeral pyres, and which had been consigned to the sacred waters.

I also saw the dead body of a child, with a wreath of yellow flowers around its neck, floating down the river. I was told that praying machines were dipped in the river and swung with solemn ceremony over the heads of devotees who had made long pilgrimages from the interior to reach the holy city of Benares. The water from the Ganges is drunk by the people all over India as sacred and most beneficial to guard against sickness and death.

Speaking of the belief of the Hindoos in the sacredness of the waters of the Ganges, I am reminded that when in Calcutta I was told that there was a devout Hindoo living in Madras, in the southern part of Hindostan, so devoted to his belief in the holiness of the Ganges water that he had brought to him from

Calcutta every day a large cask of this water. He would allow no other for drinking to be used in his household.

Next to Benares, Allahabad, called by the natives the "City of God," is considered the holiest city in existence. It is situated just at the meeting of the Jamma River with the Ganges. The Hindoos believe that there is a third invisible and celestial river, which flows direct from heaven and unites with those two rivers at Allahabad. Pilgrims are constantly coming to this place to render their devotions to this imaginary river. On their arrival, they have their heads and beards carefully shaved, and the hair is thrown into the stream. Their sacred writings promise that for every hair thus disposed of, a million of years is assured the believer in paradise.

We sometimes read in the newspapers of whole cities and towns along the Ganges being destroyed by inundations. Such calamities can well happen. One must understand, however, that the houses are not generally strong and substantially constructed, but only built of sun-dried mud. They are not expected to withstand the heavy deluges that occasionally visit that country. A destroyed town is quickly rebuilt. As soon as the rains cease the mud, or soft clay, is formed into blocks and dried in the sun, the heat being very great, and the new house is built, as it were, in a day. The walls are not more than six feet high and no interior finish is required. A house of this kind comes quickly into existence.

I could prolong my chat about Benares indefinitely had I the time, for everything one sees in this far-off land is very novel and full of interest, but I want to speak of what I saw in the north of India.

Agra and Delhi are two of the important cities in India. Agra contains "the priceless pearl and India's pride," as the *Taje-Mehälle* is called. This is a mausoleum erected by Shah Jehan in the memory of his favorite wife, called *Moomtaz-i-*

THE TAJ AT AGRA, INDIA.

Muhul, or "Exalted One of the Palace." Shah Jehan was the reigning monarch of this part of India two hundred and fifty years ago. Although there are in India other marble edifices of wonderful structure and inlaid with beautiful stones, inside and outside, nevertheless the Taje is not only the most beautiful building of that country, but is unsurpassed by any other in the world. It now shows some signs of decay produced by ruthless conquerors or by the passing touches of time. But in its original splendor and glory, the Taje was a masterpiece of architecture, matchless as a work of art; even now it is conceded to be the most exquisitely beautiful structure in existence.

It only retained its original splendor for a short period. A hostile tribe living beyond the Himalaya mountains, having heard of this magnificent pile, invaded the country with a horde of robbers, conquered Agra and sadly marred the beautiful mausoleum of which I speak, taking from its marble walls many of the precious stones inlaid therein. A description—even imperfect, it may be—of this wonderful structure in the north of India will enter our chat this evening and I am sure it will be of interest.

This building stands on a foundation of red sandstone reaching twelve feet above the ground. It is octagonal in form; in architecture it is purely Saracenic. The roof is seventy feet above the foundation; the dome is surmounted by a gilt crescent, the top of which is two hundred and sixty feet from the foundation. The dome was originally covered with plates of solid gold. The walls, outside and inside, are inlaid with coral, amethyst, blood-stone, mother-of pearl, lapis-lazuli, agates of rich colors, carnelian stone in various tints, jasper, and many beautiful stones unknown in European countries, besides rare marbles and richly gold-veined alabaster from Egypt. The more precious stones, especially diamonds and rubies, which are now gone, were placed near the base of the building, as the defaced walls indicate.

At the two entrances were originally massive silver doors, studded each one with a thousand and one hundred silver-headed nails. The plunderers tore off all the gold and silver and melted them into ingots for more easy transportation.

Neither glass nor wood nor any common metal was incorporated in this building. Both the outside and inside have the same style of ornamentation in inlaid work. The designs are largely floral and scroll work. The arches over the doors and windows, whose lines continue to the floor, are decorated with festoons and veins of convolvuli in lapis-lazuli and blood-stone. Entire chapters from the Koran are inlaid with black marble on the walls. The roses are wrought in coral and carnelian. I counted in one rose eighty pieces of shaded coral. The lilies are wrought in mother-of-pearl, with stems and leaves of blood-stone. The various species of flowers are represented by stones having the colors of the natural flowers.

The tombs of Shah Jehan and the princess are of white marble, richly decorated with mosaic. Originally there were diamonds, rubies, emeralds and turquoises as large as English walnuts set in the decorations: but nothing of this valuable inlaid work remains except the leaves, vines, and tracery work in less valuable stones.

The cost of this magnificent building, as Mr. Bayard Taylor tell us, cannot be easily estimated. Most of the labor was done by slaves, who received only a small allowance of provisions of rice, corn, fish, and wild fruits. Much of the material was contributed by neighboring tribes, and for other portions of the materials levies were made upon dependent tribes.

Although the Taje is enchanting by moonlight, it is more resplendent in the sunlight. I had the good fortune to see this marvel of beauty under most favorable circumstances. In the

A CORRIDOR IN THE PALACE AT AGRA, INDIA.

light of the early morning it was tinged with a roseate color; the white marble appeared like a pale coral; by the mid-day sun it sparkled as if studded with colored stars; in the twilight it had a soft blue shading of color. By the artificial illumination, as I saw it, its varied beauties are still more exquisite.

The Taje may be called a living poem of wondrous beauty, suggested by the "Tales of the Arabian Nights."

This mausoleum was erected in 1600. Tavernier, the renowned French traveler of his time, who records having seen the structure in process of construction, tells us that twenty thousand men were occupied seventeen years in its building. During the period of the erection of the tomb there was great mortality among the laborers, and the peasantry cried out:

"Have mercy, O God, on our distress,
For we die, too, with the princess."

Long before the tomb was finished the Princess Moomtaz died, and her remains were placed in the unfinished mausoleum; the Shah soon followed his favorite and was placed beside her in the crypt of the tomb.

Besides this mausoleum there are other beautiful marble palaces in Agra, remembrances of the age of India's glory and splendor, to describe which would make our chat too long, for there is yet more to include in this chapter on India. But I cannot forbear telling you of a very strange human being that I saw at the English mission school near Agra. He was a young man of about twenty years of age who had been taken from a wolf's den twelve years before. He was discovered in company with a she-wolf, and crept about on his hands and feet. The animal had apparently accepted the boy as her own offspring, It is supposed he had been carried off in infancy by the wolf, and had been suckled and cared for by the animal. The boy is called "Saturday," because he was discovered and captured on that day.

For some time after being reclaimed he was wild and intractable, and howled like a wolf, and appeared very unhappy away from the mother wolf; he would eat only raw meat. But gradually and by kind treatment he was taught to stand upon his feet and to walk without getting down on "all fours." But he still walked with the same awkward gait as trained quadrupeds do on their hind feet. It has required years of time and long continued patience on the part of his manager to teach him the few short words he can now utter. Although he understands the commands given him, he still makes known his wants by signs and ejaculations. His eyes have a wild look, and he keeps his lower jaw in constant motion. His face is not disagreeably ugly, although it is marked with scars, supposed to have come from the wounds made by the wolf. He is quite tame now and really very kindly disposed.

I must take my young readers as far as Delhi, although they may think they have remained long enough already in the distant land of India. Delhi is not far from the foot-hills of the Himalaya mountains, called by the natives the Halls of Snow, and is one of the principal points of commerce in the cashmere shawls so highly appreciated the world over. The shawls are brought from the mountain districts, where they are made, to this place on the backs of elephants and camels. However, they must first pass through Serinagur, a town north of Delhi, where the rajah, or governor of the province, collects a tax on every shawl manufactured for sale either at home or for exportation. From Delhi they are taken to Calcutta, the general shipping market for all Indian products.

We sometimes call India shawls camel's-hair shawls, but this is a misnomer. Shawls and cloths made of the hair of camels are very coarse and heavy, and are only used by soldiers and natives for blankets. The wool of which the fine shawls are made is from the cashmere goat of the Himalaya mountain districts.

THE KUTUB MINAR.—A CORRIDOR OF THE MOSQUE NEAR THE KUTUB MINAR, DELHI, INDIA.

is in the form of a peacock's tail with full spread feathers, the colors of the peacock plumage being imitated by the various colored precious stones set in gold. No labor or cost was spared to produce the finest gems. It was supported by six feet of massive gold and set with rubies, emeralds and diamonds. When the Shah sat upon his throne he wore a turban of cloth of gold, having a bird like a heron wrought upon it, whose feet were covered with diamonds of large size, and a large oriental topaz that shone like the sun was inserted in front of the turban.

It is said that the father of the Shah induced the manufacture of this costly throne to display the wealth of precious stones that had been amassed in the royal treasury by despoiling the rich rajahs of neighboring provinces, and from the presents which the rajahs of smaller provinces were obliged to make upon certain yearly festal days.

This throne with all its jewels is now in the possession of the Shah of Persia, and stands in the grand audience chamber of his palace at Teheran. It has been described to me by the wife of the late United States Minister to Persia, Mrs. B., who spent several years at that court. Many of the jewels are still uncut, although the larger number are cut. It is the most brilliant combination of jewels in existence.

After having seen many of these wonderful Indian palaces composed of marble and precious stones, I am half inclined to think that some of the tales of the "Thousand and One Nights" are founded on facts, and are not altogether creatures of the imagination, for the events and interior scenes of life within their walls must have been to a certain extent in correspondence with the gorgeousness of the exterior of their palaces.

THE AUDIENCE CHAMBER IN THE PALACE AT AGRA.

CHAT VIII.

CHINA.

Landing through the Surf at Madras—Wind in the Chinese Sea—Fighting a Typhoon—Gems in Natives' Ears—The Travelers' Palm—Hong Kong—In the Bungalow—Feet too Small for Walking—The Chinese Merchant is a Gentleman and Carries a Fan—The Jade Stone—Chinese Marriages—The Bride and Groom not Consulted—The Wailing Before the Marriage—Married Before She Sees her Husband—Judged by her Feet—Eating Eggs Two Years Old—Must Pay to Keep Away the Cemeteries—Burial Mounds—In the Lime Pit—A Bow-wow-wow Ragout—Confucius—His Belief and his Epitaph—The Judge who Insisted that the World was Flat—The Fatal Girdle of Silk—Boat Life in China—Children on and in the River—An Immense Empire—Rice and Silk—The Imitation Chinaman.

From the north of India we directed our course for China, and our steamer touched at Madras, in the south of Hindostan. There is no good harbor there, and because of the high surf the steamer anchored a considerable distance from the land. I was quite amused by the manner of taking on and landing passengers at that port. It was something after this wise: The person is tied in an arm chair, which is swung off by ropes running from the yard-arm in order to clear the ship, and then let down to reach a small boat which is dancing continually and wildly on the waves and dashing against the side of the ship.

While suspended over the side of the vessel waiting for a propitious wave to bring the little craft up to the right position, the passenger himself must decide the moment when to disembark from the chair, and at a word or gesture a half-dozen of the boatmen quickly grapple the side of the ship with their long iron hooks, and so steady the little boat somewhat, while others grasp the chair, from which the passenger frees himself with a nervous haste, and takes a seat as best he can in the bottom of the boat and is then rowed ashore through a heavy and foaming surf. These surf boats are quite deep and made of bark closely joined together by bamboo splints. It requires twelve men to manage one of these canoes. But notwithstanding the dangers of boarding a ship at anchor, the snake-charmers, jugglers and hucksters of all kinds of small wares do not hesitate to venture on board in the hope of picking up a few pennies.

The sea along the coast of China is subject to typhoons or hurricanes twice a year during the change of the monsoons, or trade-winds. These changes occur in the spring and autumn, after which the prevailing winds blow in one direction continually for several months. The vessels going with the winds have fair sailing, but woe to those going in the contrary direction, or to those which are caught in the change of the monsoons; for in the case of the latter the voyage is long and boisterous, and a ship which meets the change of monsoon is often lost.

Before reaching China we encountered a typhoon; it was a frightful struggle between the ship and the waves. In addition to the fury of the wind the rain was falling in blinding torrents. At times the great ship was lifted almost out of the water as a tremendous roller ploughed under her bow and sent her high up in the air; then came alongside another mountain wave and gave the ship a heavy blow, from which she would bound like a foot-ball and then settle down on one side upon her beam-ends; and again, before the ship could right herself, another immense wave would overtake the preceding one and sweep along the deck, beating her almost entirely under water; then the ship seemed to give a leap as if to free herself from the tremendous grip of the waves, and for a moment appeared to settle steadily down between two monster surges, but only to rise upon other and yet higher billows. This movement of the ship continued for hours. But the skill of the navigator triumphs over the furies of the tempest, and we are safe at last in a tranquil sea. What sensations for all on board a ship during a typhoon! Experience only can give one an idea of its terrors.

After passing Madras we touched for a short time at the island of Ceylon, noted for its cocoanut forests, and cactus jungles alive with wild animals, monkeys and beautifully plumaged birds, besides its unlimited wealth of precious stones. Many of the natives, both men and women, wear uncut and unpolished precious stones which lapidaries could manipulate into beautiful gems.

The Cingalese women wear nose rings, from which oftentimes depend pearls and uncut emeralds, or rubies and sapphires, while the men may perhaps have on each ear three pearls, or stones of value, attached to rings by means of holes drilled through them. American and European jewel dealers have their agents in Ceylon, on the lookout for the beautiful gems found there, and who procure them as soon as offered for sale.

Among the great variety of curious trees growing in these tropical countries is a species of palm found in Ceylon, which contains in the hollow stem of its leaf a sweet, green, aromatic water, cool and delicious, to quench thirst. The stem is tapped near its base, and from this incision a glassful of the refreshing liquid is obtained. The cut grows together quickly, and the stem soon fills again with the sap. This palm tree is very welcome to those traveling through the island, and hence it is called the "traveler's palm." It bears a thick, green, fan-shaped leaf.

After a generally pleasant voyage, Victoria Mountain, rising above Hong Kong, came in sight. Hong Kong is rather an English than a Chinese city, although there is a large Chinese quarter where the natives may live undisturbed after their own way of life. The city is built upon the mountain slopes, which are terraced from the water's edge half-way up the mountain side.

Upon the top of the mountain is a picturesque bungalow, or villa, in the midst of a beautiful garden where there are fruits and vegetables ripening and maturing all the year round. This bungalow is occupied by the English Chief Justice. The foreigners and better class of natives occupy bungalows; these houses are well built of wood, one story high, with a steep and high gable roof thickly thatched with straw, and surrounded on all sides with a wide veranda, provided with rolling curtains of straw matting, which are let down to exclude the sunshine during the heat of the day. The verandas are furnished with bamboo extension chairs, tables, pots of green plants, and cages of singing birds. In fact the veranda is the daily rendezvous for the family. The morning coffee and the evening tea are taken there.

Hong Kong is a large commercial city under British government. The Chinese women of rank are never seen walking in the streets. They go about in sedan chairs, quite shut in by blinds or curtains. The custom of cramping their feet out of their natural shape prevents much walking by them. Among the coolie, or working population, the women do not distort the feet; they are born to work, and must have the full use of them.

The Chinese merchant is a gentleman. He sits at a table at his ease in his little shop, and has two or three servants to do his bidding in showing articles for sale. He is dressed in a blue silk blouse, his hair is nicely plaited with artificial hair down to his feet; his fan—a Chinese gentleman must have a fan—is tucked down the back over the left shoulder and under his blouse, from whence he draws it out at his pleasure, and he can handle it quite as coquettishly as any young lady. The nails of the little fingers are allowed to grow at least a quarter of an inch from the end of the fingers. This is proof positive that he is a gentleman, and performs no manual labor. While he is affable in making sales, he is very earnest in manner and seldom smiles. To Europeans he speaks what is called "pidgin-English," which runs something as follows: The merchant we will suppose sends the servant up stairs to get a roll of silk to show to a lady customer, and he says, "Johnny, runny topside, very quickly—you sabe—and catchee me rolly silk; Melican lady buy some." Unless there is a probability of making a sale, the merchant appears very much absorbed in his counting board, (a machine with which he solves mathematical problems,) and pays but little attention to the shopper.

Of all the precious stones the Chinese prize most highly the jade stone. High officials wear a ring of white or green jade stone upon the thumb of the right hand.

The social customs of the Chinese are quite unlike those of any other people. With them marriages are celebrated in a manner peculiar to their own country. Mothers choose wives for their sons, and make the choice without consulting them as soon as they are old enough to marry. The mother is not content until the eldest son—if there is more than one son in the family—is married and has a son, or until she has a grandson, to perform the burial rite at her death.

Marriages are arranged by "go-betweens"—the rank of the parties being considered—or women who are one of four living generations of females, the second in line being eligible to serve in this capacity. The contracting parties never see each other until the bride is brought to the bridegroom's house. There is no wedding service performed by a priest; the ceremony simply consists in the preparation of the bride to leave the home of her ancestors, which takes place on the last day after a month of mourning and wailing because she is to leave her family.

The girl is not promised in marriage until one month before she leaves the paternal roof. She spends this time in mourning, weeping, and wailing in loud tones of voice. If she belongs to a family of high rank, she is allowed to absorb herself entirely for the month in this expression of grief and desolation, which is supposed to convey the idea that her unhappiness is caused on account of leaving the home of her parents. Several of her dearest maiden friends attend upon her during this period of mourning, whose pleasure it must be to join with the bride in her lamentations. A common quality of clothing is furnished to the bride for this season of preparation, which must be torn to shreds during the paroxysms of grief and wailing. If the bride is of a low and working class, she is allowed to continue in her daily avocation to a certain extent, but she must feign the sadness of the situation at least a portion of the time.

Until girls, even in all classes, are chosen for wives, they wear their hair in one long plait hanging down the back. The day the bride is to go to her new home, the same "go-between" who has arranged the marriage spends the day with the girl, and superintends the final preparations. The last thing is to comb the mass of tangled hair, which is done in a very rough manner with a coarse wooden comb, even to pulling it out in quantities, until the girl screams in real agony; it is then arranged in the coiffure of a married woman, which is a simple knot upon the top of the head.

The bride remains the entire day, from eight o'clock in the morning until the hour she leaves home, which is about six o'clock in the evening, upon a very hard bed covered with a red silk or cotton blanket, red being the mourning color. Her bridesmaids, who have been in attendance during the month of mourning, remain at her bedside and at times join in the vociferous and apparently heart-rending tones of the mourning agony, indicating that the grief of the bride is almost unbearable. The mother stands by, to all appearances an indifferent observer. The invited guests—including only women—who came at eight o'clock in the morning, remain in the room, also silent observers.

The hour approaches when the bride is to leave home; she is gaily attired, her hair has been neatly put up on the top of the head and adorned with ornamental pins, and she is allowed to leave her bed and receive the mournful salutations of the attending friends, and then she expresses the final sad good-byes to her family and young friends who have been with her during these weeks of sadness.

At five o'clock in the afternoon a simple repast is offered to the family and guests, but the bride eats nothing during the day, the custom of the country requiring the bride to go hungry to her new home.

After the wedding repast is finished, the bride is carried on the back of her ama, or maid, to the closed sedan chair which awaits her on the veranda, and followed only by the "go-between," who accompanies her by the side of the chair with a lighted lantern in hand, she proceeds to the house of her husband, for she is now married; several sedan chairs follow, containing the gifts that have been bestowed upon her. When the bride's chair leaves the house, large quantities of rice are thrown over it, which is understood to express the wish that the bride may always have plenty.

On the arrival of the bride at her new home, the husband comes to the chair, which is closed and locked, the "go-between" having the key in charge, and raps on the door a significant number of times: the signal is recognized and answered, whereupon the key is handed to the husband, who unlocks the door and the "go-between" takes the bride upon her back, wailing and screaming, thereby expressing to her husband her great sorrow at leaving the paternal roof, and carries her to the apartment she is to occupy; there she is divested of her wrappings and thick veil, and the husband looks upon the face of his bride for the first time.

The first matter of importance to the husband is the size of his wife's feet; if they are sufficiently small to please his fancy, he is well satisfied with his bride. If they are too large, then perhaps a shade of disappointment is seen on his countenance. But under no circumstances can he change the state of affairs. His only redress, if not content, is to ask his mother to find another wife for him. However, as all the personal details are arranged by the "go-between," care is taken that the fancy of the husband shall be suited.

At the end of a month the young wife may go each day to her father's house for one month if she chooses to do so, but she must return to her own home at night.

Among the low classes of Chinese there is much less ceremony concerning marriages, but the month of mourning is the essential point in any case and must be observed to a certain extent.

The above description may appear too strange to be probable, but it was related to me by a lady who had resided eight years in Canton and had attended many such weddings.

Another custom peculiar to the Chinese is their system of preserving eggs, which is supposed to keep them any length of time. The eggs are immersed in a strong decoction of an aromatic wood, and allowed to remain three days therein; then they are taken out and smeared over with a paste made of lime, salt and wood ashes, buried and left undisturbed for at least forty days.

after which they are considered fit for use. Eggs prepared in this way are highly relished by the Chinese gourmand, even after two years' keeping.

The Celestials, as the Chinese are often called, because they speak of their country as the Celestial Kingdom, have one invariable law in their social system, whose requirements under no circumstances can be ignored ; yet its decrees are subject to whim and to pecuniary conditions. It is the law of the *Feng-Shui*, which, interpreted into English, means the wind and water spirit. An intelligent native will say this law, which is a governing power with them, is called a wind and water spirit because it is like the wind, for one cannot tell whence it comes, and like the water because no one can grasp it.

This system was established in the year 1200. The adherence to the *Feng-Shui* principle has no doubt largely hindered progressive movements among the Chinese. It has not allowed the construction of railroads in China to any extent ; it will not permit the making of public roads or highways through some districts ; in fact, it does not approve any movement looking toward a departure from the old customs.

For scores of years foreigners have been trying to discover just what the *Feng-Shui* is, in order to avoid possible antagonisms in commercial affairs, but all in vain. The decree is only applicable to each individual case. A man wishing to buy a piece of land, or to establish himself in business, asks the consent of the representative official of the *Feng-Shui*. If he does not wish to grant the request he simply bows politely, and declares that on account of the *Feng-Shui* it is impossible. However, a second appeal, accompanied with an increased consideration or gift, is more graciously listened to, and after a private consultation with another official, the request may perhaps be granted. Frequently the *Feng-Shui* permits the burial mounds of the natives to be constructed near the residences of foreigners. In such a case the only protection is to get permission to build a high wall around their grounds, in order to shut out from view the unpleasant sights of Chinese cemeteries. The law of the *Feng-Shui* is very compliant, and may be induced to consent to almost anything, but concessions must always be paid for. If, however, a foreigner cannot get a concession to enclose his property, he must endure the consequences of having improvised cemeteries at his very door, and perhaps in full view.

A near prospect of these burial mounds is not agreeable. Sometimes a dead body placed in a rough box rests on the surface of the ground, being covered only with matting or straw, held down by stones heaped upon it. It is true, however, that the quick-lime thrown upon the body soon destroys the odors and decomposes the flesh and bones. Dead bodies are generally very indifferently disposed of, and are frequently left on the surface of the ground; hence the importance of using quick-lime. The Chinese also practice cremation, although less than the other method of disposing of the dead.

Until European influence began to prevail in China children were not buried even in this rough manner; they were simply thrown on some waste spot of ground and covered with lime. Whatever was left undecomposed by the lime was washed away by rain. Now they bury children more decently; a large pit is dug and covered with a bamboo roof. The body is wrapped in matting or canvass, and thrown into the pit with a quantity of lime, which quickly destroys it.

Some years ago an incident occurred in a family related to the writer which may interest you, as showing how appropriately children born far away from home may be named. While an English merchant vessel was lying at Shanghai the captain's wife, who was on board, gave birth to a daughter, whom she named "Mary, the far East." Again the captain and his wife were making another voyage and chanced to be at the Sandwich Islands, when a second daughter was born, who was called "Jane, the far West."

Another reminiscence of Shanghai may not be inappropriate just here: A party of American gentlemen having finished a very good meal at a Chinese restaurant, one of them wished to know what the savory ragout was made of from which they had freely partaken with relish. He exhausted all the "pidgin-English" terms used in a restaurant, but the Chinaman would only reply, "He very good; Melican man eat him." At last the gentleman, in a state of desperation, pointing to the smoking dish on the table, said, "He makee quack, quack, quack?" meaning to ask if it was a duck ragout. The waiter answered, "No, Melican man; he makee bow-wow-wow. No like he now, Melican man?"

Confucius was the great religious sage of China in the same sense that Mohammed is considered the source of wisdom among his followers. Confucius lived about the fifth century before the Christian era. It is estimated that a third portion of the human race are believers in the doctrines and maxims of Confucius. He attained his high position among the Chinese by the strength and purity of his character. When he had arrived at the age of full manhood he began to study the character and conduct of men; it appeared to him that they were largely governed by selfish and unworthy motives in their dealings with their fellow-men; that there was but little appreciation of right and wrong among the people, and he felt himself called by the higher power to undertake the work of moral reformation.

He commenced to teach at the age of twenty-two years. One of the first principles in his system of instruction was thoroughness in mental exercise and in self-discipline. "When I have presented," said he, "one corner of my subject, and the pupil cannot himself make out the other three, I do not repeat my lesson." On being asked by a high official in what good government consisted, according to his opinion, he replied, "When the ruler is ruler, the minister is minister, the father is father, and the son is son." Early in his teachings he already had many followers. He traveled extensively in his own country, often running great risks of his life, but he had a sense of security in his belief that he would be protected by Heaven until his career in this world should be finished.

Upon his mausoleum is the following inscription, as translated into English: "The wisest ancient teacher, the all-accomplished, all-informed king on earth."

He died at the age of seventy years, spending nearly all of his life in the improvement of the social condition of his fellowmen. He calls himself "transmitter," not a "maker" of doctrines, giving it to be understood that he received his doctrines from a Supreme Being, and through him they were given to men.

No beef is eaten by the Chinese because Confucius said it was wicked to take the life of an animal useful in agriculture.

The tenets of the *Feng-Shui*, of which I have already spoken, came into existence long before Confucius's time. In the early days of this law it was called the "Book of Changes." Even Confucius did not attempt to explain the principles of the *Feng-Shui*, nor question its oracles.

That Chinamen are carefully informed and firmly fixed in their belief there is no question, as the following incident will show: On a certain occasion a friend of the writer was presented to a judge in the court of justice at Shanghai. After the presentation ceremony was finished, the judge inquired through an interpreter what brought the gentleman so far away from his home. The reply was that he, in company with several of his friends, was making the journey around the world. Whereupon the judge questioned the possibility of a human being going *around* the world. He said the world was flat, and that the man did not live who could climb up the sky and go over on the other side; and he asked the tourist in all gravity if they did not understand in America that the world was flat!

The Chinese of the more intelligent class are moved by a high sense of honor and dignity, more than many people, perhaps, although there are doubtless many exceptions to this rule, and wicked men are found there as elsewhere. It is related of one of the ancient emperors that an invasion was made by an unfriendly tribe in his empire which resulted in the overthrow of his power, and he was in turn condemned to exile from his country. He applied to the *Feng-Shui* for advice as to what he should do under the circumstances. The official of this high power did not dare to give advice on so delicate a question, and the emperor himself decided his own fate. He conducted his beloved empress into a distant part of the garden without uttering a word. She at once understood his silent agony, and after tenderly embracing him, she retired and suspended herself by the silken girdle which she took from her waist. The emperor followed her quickly in death. He first cut off the head of his beautiful wife with his cimeter, and then with the same girdle hung himself upon another tree.

The sea coast and river shores of China are generally low and marshy, and consequently are subject to frequent inundations—hence the dreadful disasters from overflowed rivers that we sometimes read about. And while oftentimes great loss of life ensues from these inundations, great advantages also follow. The countless surface-buried dead are swept away into the sea by these overflows, which must have the grateful effect of cleansing the soil and purifying the atmosphere.

China is famous for its immense population. The people are gathered in great cities or thronged in innumerable villages in the agricultural districts. Hundreds of thousands also live in boats on the rivers, bays and harbors. This boat-life is peculiar to itself, and quite distinct from land life. These people, old or young, seldom touch foot on shore. They are born in junks, as Chinese ships are called, fulfill their mission in life on deck, and at last are buried from the stern of a boat. There are floating theatres, joss boats—as those having shrines are called—tea and dance boats inhabited by young girls, which meander constantly through the forest of boats in all the principal harbors, but always hovering close by the shores and inviting patronage from shoremen as well as boatmen. The girls marry and take perhaps only a rice-kettle, a pillow, a mat, a pair of chop-sticks, and a change of blouse for a marriage portion, and go aboard the lover's boat, perfectly satisfied with their lot in life.

These boats have awnings of matting over the stern, which are let down at night and shut in the little family circle. The daily routine of life is performed on deck in full view of their neighbors. If the family increases too fast, or number too many girls, which is considered a misfortune among the boat population, the surplus little ones, especially the females, are allowed to crawl to the side of the boat and fall off, unobserved, into the water, and are soon lost to sight. The mother, no doubt, thinks it is the will of the *Feng-Shui* that the child should not live, and is quite reconciled. When the little ones are not an encumbrance in the family they are tied at one end of a cord not long enough to admit of their getting to the edge of the boat, the other end being fastened at a proper place, and thus they are taken care of.

Among the higher class of Chinese the birth of a son is the occasion for great rejoicing. When the child is one month old the relations and intimate friends of the family send it a silver plate, upon which is engraved the words, "Long life, honors, felicity," and the name of the child in full.

China is an immense country ; the empire is estimated to be

twice the size of the United States. It has the variety of climate which yields the products of the northern latitudes as well as the vegetation of the tropics. The camphor and cinnamon trees grow without cultivation, and the tea-plant is a natural product in many parts of China, but it is greatly improved by cultivation. I have sipped tea in China which cost $20 a pound. Rice is one of the chief products of that country, being literally the staff of life for the people. The rice-pot is upon every boat, in every cabin, and in fact under every home roof in China. There the silk worm furnishes the fabric for clothing, as does the cotton plant in America.

The Chinese have a wonderful faculty for imitation. A photograph from a foreign land may be given to a portrait painter, with descriptions of the color of the eyes and hair, and the tint of the complexion, and he will reproduce a copy enlarged to life size that will be a speaking likeness. A very amusing affair occurred not long ago which reflected considerably on the Chinaman's good sense but proved his qualification as an imitator. An English officer on board a merchant ship lying at anchor off Canton desired to procure several pairs of nankin trousers. He sent a pair to the tailor as a pattern, but unfortunately there chanced to be a small patch inserted in one knee, and he forgot to inform the tailor that the patch must not appear on the new garments. In due time the half-dozen pairs of new trousers were sent on board, accompanied with a polite note which expressed the hope that the trousers would suit, as they were exactly like the model. But imagine the surprise of the officer when he discovered that every pair had a patch upon one knee, precisely like the sample pair! There was no alternative but to pay the bill and be silent.

The Chinese are very skillful in garden culture; they cultivate fruit and flowers to perfection. In public gardens may be seen some of the native forest trees, and also specimens from other countries dwarfed to two and three feet in height, and yet preserving all the peculiarities of the trees.

A Chinese house is certainly a luxury in one way at least, for it shows a way of dispensing with many of the unnecessary articles which in some countries are considered indispensable in a well-regulated household at the present day, but which add greatly to the care and labor of domestic life. Carpets, high walls, a superabundance of fine linen, elaborate furniture, costly silver and glass, the inevitable scarf that falls so easily out of place, and the thousand and one pieces of bright colored bric-a-brac seen in our dwellings, do not exist in a Chinese home; consequently the mistress of the household knows nothing of the numberless sources of fatigue and the innumerable elements of annoyance which all these beautiful component parts of a *civilized* home must cause. And yet a Chinaman's home may possess every essential for comfort, cleanliness and health. Perhaps in the rotation of time, and after every conceivable luxury has been exhausted, we, too, may accept a more primitive and simple style of home life.

And so I could continue to talk of what I saw and heard in China, but our steamer is waiting, and we must hasten on board for the next stage of our journey around the world.

CHAT IX.

JAPAN.

The Japanese not like the Chinese—How Foreigners are Treated in Japan—An Earthquake for Dessert—Walls Covered with Fans—Japanese Houses and Furniture—Chop-sticks—The Bedrooms—The Tea-Houses and the Pretty Maids—Beards for Grandfathers and Blackened Teeth for Wives—Men and Women Flying Kites—Deft Workers in Paper—Queer Notions about Saving Life—Calmly Watching his Friend's Struggles with the Waves—Cash for Prayers—Japanese Horses—The Youngsters' Somersaults—Means of Traveling—Making a Tree Look Like a Man—Boats for the Spirits of the Dead—On the Pacific—Weeks of Eastward Sailing—Halfway Across from London—Dropping and Adding a Day.

After a pleasant passage the bold and wooded shores of Japan appeared in sight with the great volcanic peak of Fusiyama, and we will devote a little time this evening to an account of a few of the many instructive and amusing objects one sees in Japan. One who has never been to these regions is likely to think that the Chinese and the Japanese are almost as one people in character and customs. But the two countries should not be considered as sister-nations, although it is but a step comparatively from one to the other. The two peoples are not at all alike in their manners and customs of life, although both belong to the Mongolian race..

Japan accepts to a certain extent the civilization of the present age; China resists all innovations upon its own national life. The Chinese are a very grave and haughty people: the Japanese are more affable in their manners and disposition. The Chinese women never appear in public; the Japanese women assist in the shops, attend to the tea-houses, and go about unveiled in open jinrickshaws—the name given to small hand-drawn carriages that are little larger than a child's carriage. The Japanese look quite graciously upon foreigners, even sitting down with them at table on dinner occasions. They do not cramp the feet as do the Chinese women. The Japanese accept more generally European education than do the Chinese; they are called the "Parisians" of the East. There are many Japanese students in our colleges, among whom are a few young women. In the larger Japanese cities certain districts are assigned to the foreign residents; they may carry on business in other portions of the cities, but they must return to their quarters at night. In many of the interior towns foreigners are not allowed to remain over night. The concession of residence to foreigners is, however, quite recent. At one time Japan was entirely closed to Europeans except at the port of Nagasaki, where the Dutch could trade. It is but thirty-five years since the first Japanese port was opened to all foreigners; now they are following along in the course of the general progress of the world, and without doubt most of them now believe with all civilized nations that the world is round, while, as we have seen, the Chinaman believes the world is flat.

One of my various experiences which occurred in Tokio, or Yeddo, the capital city of Japan, was a "tiffin," or lunch party, which took place in the Hamagoten palace, one of the Mikado's city residences. The Mikado is the sovereign of Japan. There were fifty guests at the table, among whom were two Japanese ladies who appeared in the rich toilettes of their country. The menu cards were eight inches square, of scarlet paper, with the menu printed in black Japanese characters, of which each forms a complete word. The cuisine and service of the "tiffin" was in French style, but with the dessert came an earthquake, which certainly was not arranged for by our host, a member of the Japanese cabinet. As the coffee and fruits were being served a heavy rumbling noise was heard, and in less than two seconds all of us were rushing to the outer doors. The house perceptibly rocked as the earth violently trembled, and the heavy bronze chandeliers swayed to and fro, describing almost half circles. It seemed an age before we reached the veranda. One of our party, an American, seemed more composed than the rest of the frightened guests. Later, when asked for an explanation of his composure, he said that he was suddenly reminded that twenty-three years previous to that time a terrible earthquake had occurred in Tokio, destroying a large portion of the city and many lives, and that the palace in which we were had withstood that shock, as it had many others, for it was one of the old palaces of Tokio. If all of us could only have remembered that fact we should have been quiet observers, rather than the terrified party we were. However, the excitement was of short duration, a second and lighter shock following, and then all was quiet again ; mother earth had already steadied herself, but we did not linger long over our coffee. All were anxious to reach their homes or temporary residences.

In the palace where this scene took place is a large room, about fifty feet square, called the "fan chamber." The only pieces of furniture in it were two magnificent cabinets of lacquer-work and four large bronze vases, one in each corner of the room. The walls were covered with fans of every conceivable shape and design. The palace was but one story high, as are all the palaces and most of the houses of residents, on account of the frequent and oftentimes severe earthquakes.

The buildings in Tokio are low and have wooden ceilings, no plaster being used in their construction. A tremor of the earth would cause plaster to fall from the walls, while ceilings of wood spring apart and unite again under the quick movement of earthquakes.

A description of the ordinary Japanese house may be of interest. It consists of a bamboo frame about sixteen feet square and fourteen feet high, the roof and four sides being thatched closely with rice straw. If the house has been built several years, small bushes and tufts of long grass may be seen creeping out on the roof and along the outer edges. Sometimes beds of bright-colored flowers mixed with grass are seen on the sloping roofs. The house is surrounded with a veranda perhaps four feet wide. This dwelling may be divided into small apartments by means of movable screens covered with painted paper and reaching almost to the ceiling. These screens are moved about to suit the convenience of the family, or for a special occasion may be removed, making one square room of the whole. The Japanese, as a race, are small in stature, and as they require but little furniture, it can be readily understood how a house of the above dimensions may serve their necessities.

The windows are sliding frames divided into several small squares and neatly covered with thin white rice paper, which admits a soft and very agreeable light, but must be renewed often, as rain soon destroys the paper panes. However, the projecting roofs half cover the verandas and serve as a great protection to these frail windows. No chimneys are required; an opening in the outer wall of the cooking department permits the escape of smoke from the small charcoal furnace used. The house needs but little furniture. A cooking furnace, a rice-pot and tea-kettle, a few cups and saucers, a small clock, a family idol, a red-cushioned movable platform

JAPANESE BED-ROOM SCENES.

about two feet high and wide enough for a number of persons sitting back to back, which serves as a seat for family and guests, and the house is furnished.

Chop-sticks, which are long, slender pieces of wood, and fingers serve for conveying the food to the mouth when at table, and small wooden or china bowls take the place of plates. Their bedroom is just as simple and primitive. A cotton mat laid upon the floor and a little wooden box covered with a cushion of rice paper, with a drawer in which to keep the toilet articles, is all that is required in the way of furniture. The covering used is a large sacque-shaped padded garment, which is put on at night. The bedroom articles are stowed away on a shelf during the day, and the room serves as a reception or living room. A small stationary tub filled with running water, standing outside the dwelling, answers for the daily ablutions of the entire family.

The tea-houses in Japan take the place of restaurants in our country ; they are to be met with everywhere in the country and in the towns. The cushioned platform, the steaming tea-kettle, a few pretty cups and saucers, the pot of smoking hot rice, and two or three pretty and coquettish tea maids are the only requirements of a restaurant. If the customer is a foreigner no price is set upon the refreshment taken, but the smiling *moosmies,* or attendants, bow very low and gracefully, and indicate by their simplicity of manners, together with an invitation to come again, that you may pay next time, or that one may pay what he pleases. These pretty and smiling maidens like very much to "air" the few English words they may chance to know, for they are ambitious to learn something of that language. One day an American dropped into a certain tea-house where he had been several times before. He always had a little dog with him on these visits, and by way of discipline, if the dog ran about too much, he would say, "Come here." The tea maids supposed this to be the name of the dog, and on this occasion one of them said to the gentleman as she handed him his cup of tea, "What a nice dog American man's 'Come Here' is; I like that name."

A Japanese family of the middle class may travel with but little baggage, as each member has only one suit of clothing, which is worn until it is necessary to replace it with another.

Among the Japanese no man is allowed to wear a beard until he becomes a grandfather; hence old bachelors must remain beardless. A girl blackens her teeth as soon as she is married; she must keep them black the rest of her lifetime.

One of the variety of amusements the Japanese indulge in and greatly enjoy is that of flying kites. Both men and women among the high and low classes engage in this sport. The kites are large or small, according to the circumstances of those taking part in the exercise. They go to the hills and high grounds in the vicinity of the cities and towns at certain seasons of the year, where they gather by the hundreds of all classes and ages; all enter into the sport actively or as spectators. Some of the kites are very large and of curious shapes and covered with grotesque paintings.

In order to avoid entanglement of lines, which would prevent the successful ascension of any of them, as there may be scores of kites flying together, the cords are dusted with powdered glass, so that if they are likely to become embarrassed or tangled in rising, the weaker lines are soon cut by the stronger and more powerful ones, and consequently must come down, leaving the kites to go off at random, while the larger ones continue gracefully soaring and manageable for a time; but while the victors are sailing beautifully on, they, too, may encounter other lines still heavier than their own, and meet with a fate similar to that which befel the weaker kites.

The sport of kite-flying consists in the struggle for supremacy among the larger kites, the liability of confusion of lines, and the frequent cutting of them, allowing the kites to wander off unmanageable in all directions. Rightly to enjoy the sport one must be provided with a number of kites, for he may lose one as soon as he lets it fly. The largest kites, of course, carry the strongest lines and make their way above the smaller ones, remaining longer afloat. The cords are wound upon reels, which are fastened at certain distances one from the other. The women take an active part in the sport, while the children are spectators.

There is wonderful skill and deftness exhibited among the Japanese in constructing curious devices of paper, and for unique designs in painting them. If they indicate a small idea of exact perspective, they know at least how to give a rich coloring to their work. In the manufacture of light and graceful fans the Japanese especially excel. Their fans are in demand the world over. Pocket handkerchiefs and napkins made of paper are in universal use ; a roll of paper handkerchiefs may be seen in the girdle of a Japanese lady.

The Japanese have very peculiar notions in regard to saving the lives of their fellows. They will not rescue human beings, who may be in peril, unless they intend or are willing to make it their pleasure to maintain such rescued ones afterward, even though it may be entirely in their power to go to their aid. And besides, they maintain that it is wrong to thwart the intentions of Divine Providence. A Japanese does not generally appreciate life in the same sense that we do.

A circumstance confirming the above was witnessed from a hotel window in Yokohama. This hotel is situated on the *bund* or quay of Yokohama Bay. At the time of the occurrence of the incident the sea was very rough and the waves were running high. There were several *sampans*, or small row boats, pulling bravely over the heavy surf to reach the shore. In one of the boats were two men, one of whom had been washed overboard by a large roller. He was soon struggling desperately to catch hold of the boat as it was dashing over the waves, while his companion sat, oars in hand, calmly looking on, but, as if moved by an impulse of mercy, he did not pull away from the drowning man. At last a huge wave caught up and tossed the sinking man into the boat. There was an unmistakable expression of happiness on the comrade's face when he saw this rescue by the merciful wave. It was evident the two men were friends, and yet one would not make an effort to save the other.

One day in my perambulations about Yokohama, unattended and alone, I saw a widow engaged in the funeral service of her deceased husband. She and the priest were kneeling and praying before an idol in one of the principal temples. The priest held a bell rope in one hand, and from time to time rang out some doleful sounds from a large bronze bell suspended over his head. In the other hand he had small pieces of wood and paper inscribed with prayers upon both sides. As he successively read the prayers he laid the several pieces of wood and paper upon the floor. When a prayer was finished the mourning widow would throw down several *cash*—copper coins of the least value in Japanese money. At last the widow arose to leave, but the priest rang the bell, and she again knelt down, when he read another prayer and she threw down a few more *cash*. The service being finished the widow went mournfully away and the priest turned toward me, and, observing that I had been a witness of the funeral ceremony, politely saluted me and departed with a smile on his countenance.

The Japanese horses are obstinate beasts. They will not move until the "bettoes," or leaders—one at the head of each horse—jerk them smartly by the bits and then start off on a

A JINRICKSHAW AND CHINESE BARBER.

run, yelling and pulling the animals after them. After two or three minutes of this violent effort, the animals go along well enough, and the "betto" jumps on a little platform at the back of the carriage. In going through villages the "bettoes" run at the heads of the horses, bounding and jumping with the steps of the animals, and yelling to clear the road from the children which may be seen playing in the dust. At the sound of horses coming along the road a troop of little naked youngsters, from three years old to children ten and twelve years of age, run into the road to meet the carriages in the expectation of getting a few *cash* for turning somersaults, which they do quite expertly, calling out at the same time "*O-hi-o*," the Japanese word for "good-morning." These little athletes ran after us by the dozen when making an excursion in the country, turning over and over like balls, and kicking up such a dust that at last we were glad to buy them off with some *cash* pieces before they started in again with their somersaults.

Traveling in the interior of Japan is done mostly by jinrickshaws drawn by two or more men, according to the roughness of the road. In many portions of the country there are no carriage roads and all journeying is done either in jinrickshaws or kangs—the latter a kind of basket in which the passenger takes a half recumbent position and is carried by means of a pole attached to each side of the basket. Four coolies will carry a man sixty miles in one day, if they are allowed to rest a few minutes occasionally to get a drink of *sacci*, or rice wine, and some boiled rice and raw fish.

The flower and fruit culture in Japan is exceedingly interesting to the foreigner. One sees a great variety of semi-tropical flowers growing luxuriantly and bearing richly-colored blossoms, but they are without fragrance; even the rose is not as fragrant there as in lower latitudes; one also sees beautiful foliage-shrubs with leaves tinged with every color of the rainbow. The Japanese are greatly skilled in a peculiar kind of tree culture. I have seen pear and apple trees dwarfed down to the size of a small rose bush of perhaps three feet in height from the ground, and laden with fruit but little smaller than the usual size. They train a certain species of evergreen tree to the shape of a bird cage, or of a coupé with a pair of horses attached; and I have seen a tree growing in the shape of a man, in which case colored plates were inserted in the head of the tree in imitation of eyes; many other curious shapes are also brought out by them in tree-growing.

Among Japanese superstitions there is one that is especially curious. They believe that the spirits of the dead come once a year, on a certain day in the month of August, to visit the sacred shrines in the temples. They do not claim to know whence they come, but they are received with music, illuminations and curious ceremonies, and on the following morning at the dawn of day they are escorted by long processions of priests and people to the water's edge, and are sent in beautiful miniature paper boats to float off whence they came.

And now, my dear traveling companions, we have only to cross in imagination the Pacific ocean, then continue our journey four thousand miles over the continent of North America, and I have brought you home with me to a pretty little town on the Hudson river.

The transit of the Pacific ocean was made without unpleasant adventure; a favorable trade wind aided the steamer, and the voyage was quickly over. The sky was blue, the sea serene and the time passed rapidly. The voyage occupied twenty-five days, and was most agreeable, with the single exception of the loneliness of our situation. For the first twenty-one days of our crossing we saw not a sail; sky and water, and sea-birds, whose companionship we had all the way over, were all we could see beyond our own ship.

During the last three days of our voyage we saw several steamers and merchant ships plowing through the waves. From time to time during our three weeks' sailing, "solitary and alone" over the great deep, I asked myself if it were possible for the ship's navigator to have lost his way! But then I reflected that we had forty-eight hundred miles to make from shore to shore, which must inevitably take weeks to accomplish.

However, we did have a break in the monotony of our voyage; at least, we had a new topic for conversation. The occasion was when we crossed the one hundred and eightieth degree of longitude from Greenwich, and were of course just half way around our globe, counting the distance from London. With us it was in the afternoon, while our friends in London at that very moment were in their beds asleep.

The traveler on his first voyage across the Pacific is not a little perplexed in trying to comprehend the calculation of time on the one hundred and eightieth meridian. When we think we understand it, we are still unable to explain it to another, or even to think intelligently about it. According to the nautical almanac we drop a day in the calendar in going from America to Japan, which puts us right with the time on that coast, and we add a day on the return voyage, in order to find ourselves in correspondence with the correct time in America. This is because in going east around the world we meet the sun, and gain a little over an hour with every thousand miles of eastward progress.

CHAT X.

HOME ONCE MORE.

Entering at the Golden Gate—Ponce De Leon—The Land of Flowers—The Fountain of Youth—Discovering a Continent—In a Country of Progress—What the Land Brings Forth—A Hotel Like a Moorish Palace—The Alligators—The Balmy South—The Great Cataract of Niagara—The Waters of Mighty Lakes—A Murderer's Hand-over-Hand Escape to Liberty—A Tight-Rope Walker Over an Awful Abyss—Submerged Shores—A Lake's Sudden Chill—A Wall of Water—The Valley of Wonders—Cascades Leaping from Mountain Heights—Where the Clouds Rest—The Virgin's Tears—The Hot and Spouting Springs—The Laughing Waters—The Arrow-maker's Daughter and Her Noble Brave—The Story of an Indian Maiden.

In our last evening's chat we were in Japan and on the waters of the broad Pacific. After a safe and pleasant voyage we at last heard the pleasant cry of "Land ho!" from the mast-head and soon were able to see from the deck the shores of America. We entered the Golden Gate, the name given to the noble harbor of San Francisco, and soon stepped foot again on our own country. While we are speeding as fast as steam can carry us across the great continent of which so large a portion belongs to the United States, let us in imagination consider some of the chief points which occur in this scenery and mark its early history.

We read that Christopher Columbus crossed the Atlantic ocean in 1492, discovered land, the Island of San Salvador, one of the Bahama group of Islands in the West Indies, and landed there; and we also read that it was reserved for one of the companions of his second voyage—Juan Ponce de Leon, a Spaniard—to discover in 1572 the peninsula now known as Florida. He sailed from Porto Rico with an expedition of three small vessels, with the intention of making a more thorough search for land in the waters looking toward the setting sun, as he was fully persuaded there was land beyond what had already been discovered. He hoped also to find a short passage to the East Indies. He therefore directed his little fleet more to the westward, not wishing to land at Cuba. On the occasion of his previous voyage he had heard enough from the natives of Cuba to convince him that there was land as yet unknown to the European, in the near vicinity of the Island of Cuba. His hopes and expectations were realized.

After weeks of tossing on the rough waters and an almost discouraging search at last he descried land. It was on Palm Sunday, in the month of April, when he landed his small, disheartened and half-famished crew near the spot where the city of St. Augustine now stands. He saw all about him on the shore such a luxuriant growth of flowers and vegetation that he at once named the place Florida, which signifies the Land of Flowers. He raised a cross near the spot where he landed, and took possession of the country in the name of his sovereigns, Ferdinand and Isabella.

Ponce de Leon learned from the natives soon after he landed in Florida that there was a great lake of medicinal water and many marvelous springs back in the interior of the country; and what was more remarkable, that there was one large spouting spring called the "Fountain of Youth," which was said to restore one to the freshness of youth, and preserve one in perpetual health by the daily use of its waters. He, with his companions, made various expeditions of many miles into the interior, where they found various large pools of water supplied by springs clear as crystal. But the so-called spring of the "Fountain of Youth" was not reached by Ponce de Leon. After many discouragements, and broken in purse and spirit, he was obliged to return to Porto Rico, leaving Juan Perez di Ortubia to continue the search after the mystic fountain of Bimini. Guided by a wise but wrinkled old woman, Juan Perez succeeded in reaching the far-famed "Fountain of Youth." But, alas! they did not experience the wished-for return of their lost youth. But if Ponce de Leon did not discover what he sought, he found Florida and the great continent of America.

This voyage was in fact the pioneer movement in the discovery of the great Western continent, and the introduction of the white man in this new land of promise, as America has come to be considered, for Columbus only discovered the outlying islands and the way across the Atlantic ocean.

The history of the discovery and occupation of America is intensely interesting to the American, young or old, not only because it is of such recent date among the world's histories of countries, but also for another important reason: because so much of its development and progress have been effected in the time of our own fathers and mothers, and we may say even in our own days. The spirit of progress as it now exists, especially in America, is moving everything on and on beyond the power of imagination. What another quarter of a century will bring about can indeed be scarcely imagined, for it would seem that everything which human genius can invent has already been accomplished.

But why should there not be a continued movement among men, as well as the constant change which is observable among inanimate matter? Does not the globe upon whose surface we live rotate daily upon its axis? And are we not told that it also makes its yearly circuit around the sun? Then we must believe that inactive matter does not exist; certainly, in the achievements of the human race there is no cessation of development. May we not, therefore, with perfect propriety indulge now and then in a degree of pride as to some of the particular achievements of the American people?

Our country received as its birthright some grand natural advantages, perhaps, over other countries, and it would seem that the spirit of enterprise born in the land rivals to a certain extent our wonderful material possessions, which are seemingly inexhaustible. We have our mines rich in ore, some of which have been discovered only within ten years, and yield enormous quantities of wealth; we have our uncounted acres of land, sending forth grains, cotton and other products to the old world; we have our natural oil wells, which, besides lighting our own country, help to illuminate many other lands; we have our sea products, such as oysters and salmon, which are shipped to other shores; we have our gas springs, which serve to give heat as well as illumination in our houses. It would seem that as a need were felt nature comes at once to our aid and supplies it. All these stores of wealth have been developed by the spirit of enterprise which is active in all parts of our land. And without doubt there is yet enough of hidden treasure to inspire effort for generation after generation to come.

As to the dates of the wonderful discoveries, and of the different progressive changes which have taken place in this country during the last fifty years, we have no time this evening to repeat them in detail. We can only get an idea of some of the geographical points in our beloved land, such as might be observed by one rapidly passing over it. I saw in my wanderings in Florida a beautiful building situated in St Augustine, the point from which we start on our rambling journeys, called the "Ponce de Leon Hotel." It is somewhat like a Moorish palace in its architecture. There are two beautiful fountains in the gardens. Alas! they do not give forth the waters of "Perpetual Youth."

Florida has been for long years the home of the alligator; but the irrepressible sportsman, finding its skin greatly sought for leather, is encroaching rapidly upon its domain, and it will not be long before the alligator will be no more, or scarce to find.

Florida is the Riviera or health resort of America, and thousands fly from the ice-bound regions of the North to enjoy its genial winter climate.

As we go northward we come to some of the wonderful water-falls for which our country is celebrated. Chief among them is the great horseshoe-shaped cataract called Niagara, falling over a precipice 164 feet in height. It precipitates in its fall, it is estimated, one hundred millions of tons of water per minute, and is one of nature's most sublime works.

Niagara is an Indian name: translated into English it means "Thunder of Waters." Niagara river is the upper outlet for the lakes Michigan, Superior, Huron and Erie, whose waters are gathered from the great streams caused in part by the melting snows of the northwest country, and carries this immense body of water over the falls to the lower lake of Ontario, and thence by the river St. Lawrence to the sea.

There are accounts of some singular adventures and narrow escapes from death, occurring in the cases of men going deliberately or falling accidentally into the rapids and over the falls.

Many years ago a murderer made his escape from the hands of justice by dragging himself hand-over-hand across the wires of an old bridge at Lewiston, near Niagara. The sheriff was behind him, the river before him, his only means of escape being

NIAGARA FALLS.

to cross the stream by the wires. He began the fearful passage; soon his hands blistered and bled, and he rested them from time to time by suspending himself from the wires by his feet. At last he reached the opposite shore and fell upon the ground as if dead. There he lay still for a short time, and then continued his flight into the wilds of the forest, and so in this fearful manner escaped arrest.

More lately Monsieur Blondin, a Frenchman, accomplished some wonderful balancing-feats while walking across the Falls on a rope. He seemed to be perfectly at his ease standing on a single rope stretched across that terrible abyss. He would sit down or lie on the rope, apparently as sure of his safety as if he were standing on firm ground. He also was able to exercise his hands in a variety of positions while suspended over the roaring waters of Niagara. Blondin still lives. Quite recently he performed some remarkable feats on the tight-rope at the Crystal Palace, near London; among other exploits this daring performer rode on a bicycle over a rope not two inches in diameter.

It is also related that from time to time some strange freaks of nature have taken place in the waters of Lake Ontario. About forty-five years ago the lake suddenly became disturbed without warning and rose more than three feet above its usual level, covering the low lands on both the Canadian and American shores and washing away all the land and buildings that obstructed the way of the rising flood. In a few days the waters receded somewhat, but never to the original water line, and consequently much of the inundated land has never been reclaimed. The reason for this disturbance and the rising of the lake has never been clearly explained; but the cause was generally supposed to be a volcanic eruption in the bottom of the lake. At another time the temperature of the water became unusually cold and the shores were covered for days with dead fish.

This occurrence at Lake Ontario reminds us of a most remarkable fact in regard to the tides in the Bay of Fundy. This bay sets back from the Atlantic Ocean between New Brunswick on the north and Nova Scotia on the south ; its tides often rise quite sixty feet, the highest-known tide on the face of the earth—a wall of water higher than many houses. Navigation in this water is at times very difficult, as may easily be imagined.

Another of the natural wonders of the country is the Yosemite Valley and its waterfalls. This gigantic mountain gorge seems to have been introduced upon the face of the earth by a convulsion in the Sierra Nevada range of mountains, which takes its rise to the southeast of the great abyss, and continues in its irregular course until it reaches the Yosemite Valley region ; there the mountains apparently end in a vast chasm. This valley should be named the Valley of Wonders, by reason of its surpassingly picturesque and sublime scenery. It is about ten miles long and one and one-half miles wide, and receives various waterfalls, which roll over the mountain sides on either hand of the great canyon or gorge and from the Merced river.

The Yosemite fall is a beautiful cascade leaping over a precipice of two thousand six hundred and thirty-four feet, broken only twice in its descent. Another beautiful waterfall is the Bridal-Veil Fall, called by the Indians Po-ho-no, meaning in their language the "Spirit of the Evil Wind." But this is not a suitable name for it, as one easily sees on beholding its entrancing beauty. Such a glorious creation should not carry the idea of anything evil, but rather convey the sentiment of something lovely and propitious. But what is in a name? This waterfall is one of nature's most beautiful pictures ; it descends gracefully and gently in one unbroken sheet of smooth water over a precipice of nine hundred and forty feet. It has been named by the white man the "Bridal-Veil Fall" because of the resemblance of the gently-falling, fan-shaped cascade to a flowing bridal veil. A brilliant rainbow forms just above the basin of the falls, when the rays of the sun strike upon the waters, giving the effect of a beautiful diadem of precious stones for the Bridal Veil.

The highest point in the Yosemite range of mountains is called "Cloud's Rest." It surmounts an almost vertical wall seven thousand feet high. The ascent may be made by a winding path on horseback, but it is a very fatiguing excursion.

There is another majestic cataract in this valley, called the "Virgin's Tears." This sheet of water tumbles over a steep of rock one thousand feet high, broken several times by jutting rocks. But wherefore this name I cannot tell.

The Yosemite valley country has but recently been disclosed to the admiration of civilized man. It was in 1851 that the first white man entered this canyon ; in 1855 the irrepressible tourist made his first appearance. Until the way was opened somewhat, access to the valley was fraught with many difficulties. There was the Indian to overcome, a trail to make out, the hardships and uncertainties of unknown roads to endure ; at any moment one was in peril of meeting the wild and unfriendly denizens of the forest. But all these obstacles to travel in the Yosemite valley and its surrounding country are now removed, and charming excursions are made in that region by tourists to California.

In the vast northwest territory of our continent there is still another remarkable phenomenal feature of land and water, the Geysers and the Hot Spouting Springs. The three principal geyser regions in the world are in Iceland, in New Zealand and in Wyoming Territory in America. The word "geyser" comes from the old Icelandic language, and means gushing or spouting. Geysers exist in many volcanic regions. In Wyoming there are hundreds of these hot spouting springs. The most wonderful one in this group lifts its spray to a height of two hundred and fifty feet. These springs cover a very large area of ground: one of them is known as the "Giantess," because of the immense bulk of water constantly spouting out; it lifts a column of boiling water two hundred and nineteen feet high. Some geysers also throw up at times masses of rock and mud, accompanied with frightful explosions. These springs send up an almost endless number of jets of steam and water.

It was in 1870, I believe, that the first exploring expedition went out into the Yellowstone park region, the hitherto almost unknown country, when that immense and wonderful desert waste, full of smoking and boiling hot springs, was discovered.

A passing allusion to the Falls of St. Anthony, or the Minnehaha Cascade, may not be uninteresting at this time. "Minnehaha" is interpreted to mean "Laughing Waters." This cascade is a gentle fall of water, over a rocky cliff more than sixty feet high. Under the illumination of the sunbeams, which causes a brilliant iridescence on the foamy waters of Minnehaha, a picture may be seen exceeding in beauty anything the deftest hand can put on canvass. A more enchanting waterfall than the Minnehaha cascade cannot be imagined.

There is a pretty legend in connection with the falls of St. Anthony, which Longfellow has immortalized in verse. The legend relates that the father of Minnehaha was an arrow-maker and had his cabin close by the cascade. One day the Good Spirit sent him a gift—a little pappoose. As the little wee winsome spirit grew in her beauty, she was named after the beautiful cascade whose waters danced gaily before his door and with their spray kept the grass always green.

One day a noble brave was on his way to the arrow-maker's hut to get a quiver of arrows; he chanced to see the dark-eyed maiden sitting on the bank of the river, bathing her feet in its curling waves. He paused a moment to catch a glimpse of her beautiful face as it was mirrored on the water, and then passed rapidly on his way lest he should be discovered by the girl.

Hiawatha returned to his people with his quiver of arrows, but not forgetting the lovely vision he saw reflected on the water he soon retraced his steps to the enchanted waterfall.

> "With his moccasons of magic,
> At each stride a mile he measured,"

and never ceased his haste until he came within sound of the cascade. He quickly reached the arrow-maker's wigwam and threw from his shoulder at the feet of the father the deer which he had killed on the way, saying he had come to ask in marriage the fair Minnehaha. The story goes that the father extended to the brave Hiawatha the hand of welcome, and replied, "Yes, if the 'Laughing Waters' wishes to go with you." "But what saith the maiden fair?" asked the wooing Hiawatha. Minnehaha timidly arose and putting her beaded blanket over her bare shoulders advanced to Hiawatha, her face tinged with the color of the rose, and with outstretched hands said, "Minnehaha will follow her noble brave." The two started at once on their bridal tour to the far-off home of Hiawatha.

I am quite sure that a more thorough study of the great waterfalls and the immense inland waters of our country would prove most instructive as well as interesting to my young readers. There are also several immense caves and grottos, or underground phenomena, in America, whose description merits careful reading, or if possible a visit in person. The wonders of our own country are not yet entirely explored, and they offer many a treat even for those who have seen the Old World.

FRAGMENTARY LETTERS.

UTAH.

SALT LAKE CITY, July 5. We made a détour of two hours by rail from the direct California route to visit the capital city of the Mormons. Somebody selected a rich and arable tract of land when this site was chosen on which to build a new Jerusalem. Salt Lake City nestles quietly in a fertile valley at the base of the range of snow-capped mountains. By irrigation the soil is rendered extremely productive. Little purling rills of snow-water from the mountains traverse the streets in all directions. We attended a Sunday service at the Tabernacle yesterday. There were present probably not less than five thousand people, this number equaling the capacity of the building. Two-thirds of the audience were women and children. One of the eminent of the twelve apostles delivered an impromptu discourse. He took no text. He exhorted the people to be faithful to the good cause which they had espoused, and assured them that there were many evidences of the prosperity of the Mormon Zion in Utah and elsewhere. He advised them to go on with the work more courageously than ever. The sermon was short. Much of the service consisted of congregational singing led by a choir of a hundred voices, accompanied, if not by the largest, certainly by the second largest organ in the country. The communion service is celebrated every Sunday. The twelve apostles break the bread and serve it with water, the latter taking the place of wine. The water is dipped from two large casks near the altar. The entire Mormon congregation, including the children, partake of the communion. The women, especially the elder ones, were attired in the oddest styles of clothing imaginable, their dresses and bonnets being exceedingly old-fashioned, to say the least, and representing the styles of many European countries, while some of the younger women were gayly dressed in New York fashions, although somewhat antiquated. The Mormons place great stress on the rites of baptism and communion. They allow themselves to be baptized frequently, and also baptize the living for the dead. Under certain circumstances they permit themselves to be "sealed" in matrimony to the dead, in which case they do not marry with the living. Brigham Young, the patriarch of the Mormons, had eighteen wives (perhaps not all of them now in good standing with the saints), and forty-nine living children. We were introduced to several of his wives and children.

CALIFORNIA.

San Francisco, July 9. The scenery along the pass in the Sierra Nevadas, through which the railroad runs from Salt Lake City to San Francisco, is majestic even to sublimity. For hours we rode through natural openings in the mountains of rocks utilized by the skillful engineer for the path of the steam-horse, and in which the ravines between the mountains are spanned by trestle-bridges. Sometimes we went curving around a rocky projection, on one side of which was a precipice more than a thousand feet deep, on the other an acclivity hundreds of feet high. Again we were shooting through a narrow pass, the sides of which were far too high to get even a glimpse of the summits of the rugged mountains. The scenery at and near "the divide" was grandly imposing; there were mountains of huge rocks, deep gorges, and eminences of sharp, smoothly cut stone, variegated with all the colors of the rainbow, seemingly the handiwork of a nation of giants. Some of the peaks of the Sierras are over ten thousand feet high. Traveling for hours through such a barren, rugged country, we seemed to be daringly encroaching on Nature's private domain. It is a wonderful work of bold engineering, this pathway of travel and commerce through the Sierra Nevadas. An open platform car is attached to the train, to afford the traveler an unobstructed view of the pass. Before reaching "the divide" we passed through twenty miles of snow-sheds. We had an artist on the train who was almost beside himself in enthusiastic admiration of the scenery, and I must confess that I was likewise affected by the sublime grandeur of these mighty works of Nature.

July 28. Here is an epitome of a two days' visit at a mansion in Alameda, a few miles from San Francisco: The estate comprises one hundred and twenty acres, every rod of which is under the highest state of cultivation possible. It contains a fine driving-park, acres of flowers, an extensive, beautifully kept lawn shaded by majestic old live oaks, and acres more of the choicest fruit. There are eight beautiful carriages and twelve blooded horses at the service of the family. The house has a corps of eighteen servants. Gas is made on the premises, and the house and grounds are brilliantly illuminated. The property extends to the San Francisco Bay, where one finds two beautiful little gondolas, with gondoliers in picturesque costumes ready for service. The main entrance-hall is eighteen by forty feet. The second-story hall corresponds to the one on the first-story, and is used as a picture gallery. Into the third-floor hall open the bedrooms, the doors of which are faced with mirrors, so that at first sight the hall appears like a salon of mirrors rather than a serviceable bedroom corridor. The halls are lighted by twenty large chandeliers. The library, on the first-floor, is much larger than the hall, and contains three thousand five hundred carefully-chosen books, and is superbly furnished. The dining-room is a companion room to the library. One end of this room is occupied by a sideboard having a mirror which extends to the ceiling and of the same width as the sideboard. Two large rooms are devoted to the amusements of billiards and bowling. The drawing-room is not yet finished and exceeds all the other rooms in size. The inside wood-work for the entire house was made in New York, and is mostly of choice imported woods. The furniture is made to match the wood-work of each room. To us were assigned two adjoining rooms of immense proportions, so large indeed that I could almost lose myself in serpentining around the massive furniture. These rooms contained every convenience and luxury belonging to bedrooms. The house service is performed by Chinamen, who move noiselessly about the house in cork-bottomed shoes. They present really a picturesque appearance in blue silk or cotton blouses, all of them having braids of plaited hair reaching down to their heels.

The lady of the mansion is a Quaker, a perfect mistress of her house, and a most charming hostess. The master is a highly cultivated and most agreeable host.

We saw bushels of choice fruit lying upon the ground. It was decaying and untouched because it was so abundant it could not be used by the family. Nothing is sold from this place—it is beneath a California king to sell fruit! This is one of three equally magnificent estates which we have visited since we came to San Francisco.

We are delighted with the Golden Gate City. The climate is delightful; even the most sensitive constitution can find here an agreeable atmosphere. One can dress thick or thin in the house; the only precaution necessary is to wear a wrap when going out to drive or walk. Even sealskin jackets are not out of place on a July day at the approach of evening, for with it comes the cool, bracing sea air. It is said the summer breezes in San Francisco are more to be feared than the winter rains.

There is almost a wasteful abundance of fruit in this city. It is sold at a merely nominal price. Choice vegetables and Oregon salmon are sold in the markets for trifling sums in comparison with the prices paid for them in the East. There are three crops of figs a year, and strawberries are to be had every month in the year. The flower gardens are in perpetual blossom from January to January. The heliotrope and fuchsia grow luxuriously enough to shade the windows and cover the verandas. There is no copper coin current here; the smallest coin used is the silver half-dime. About the lowest price for anything is a "bit," equal to ten cents.

July 31. We have made the inevitable drive to the Cliff House. It is a favorite resort for pleasure-driving. The house is located on a ledge of rocks jutting out into the sea, where there is a good view of the colony of seals. On a group of large rocks, rising high out of the water, scores of seals, old and young, disport themselves without fear of molestation. The patriarch of the colony answers readily to his name when a piece of bread is thrown to him. It is quite an infatuating amusement to watch the movements of the seals. We were as reluctant to leave the spot as children are to go away from a cage of monkeys. Quite near the Cliff House is the Lone Mountain Cemetery. The mountain is isolated, looming up out of the sandy beach ; hence its name. Since it has been occupied as a cemetery every foot of soil has been made fertile for the growth of plants and flowers by irrigation. Large trees are now perfectly "at home" on the sandy sea-shore. With its mountain of flowers the cemetery stands out in bold relief, the sea washing its base on one side. There is a magnificent park of two thousand acres, fronting the sea with miles of fine drives. By irrigation the beach along the main drive has been rendered fertile for the growth of trees, shrubbery, and the grass of lovely lawns.

We dined the other day with a friend whose house is a gem of art and beauty. The dining-room, especially, is worthy a description. Its furniture and the flooring and all the other wood-work are from foreign countries. To particularize : The parquet floor, which is wrought out of a variety of woods in beautiful designs, the doors, the frieze, and dados were made in Switzerland ; Italy contributed the statuary, the paintings and the marble mantel-pieces ; the table-service came from Dresden and Bohemia. Two Sévres vases and several bronze pieces were brought from Paris. The sideboard was manufactured in Hamburg. The dining-table and chairs were imported from England. Every article in this room is of foreign origin. It would seem that sending to Europe for fine woods is like "taking coals to Newcastle," for in California are to be found as finely-grained and richly-colored woods as can be found in any country, and skilled labor for wood-working can be obtained as readily in America as in foreign countries. Nevertheless these California Monte-Cristos have expended their money in Europe!

We have indeed much to boast of in our own country. It has the largest trees, the largest cave, the largest cataract, and the largest geyser spring in the world, and now I hear it possesses the largest pearl ever found. Not long ago, a poor Mexican fisherman, at a small seaport, dredged up a large oyster, and, to his great astonishment, found it contained a magnificent pearl. It is pure white, oval in shape, more than an inch and a half long by about one inch broad. Experts have pronounced it to be the finest pearl ever discovered. The poor fisherman wants several thousand pounds sterling for it. How much of this pearl story is true I do not know, but it is widely circulated here.

JAPAN

Yokohama, September 27. After "tiffin" at noon to-day we started for a drive. Our vehicle was a *jinrickshaw*, a two-wheeled cart, shaped like a child's hand-carriage, with a canvass hood drawn half over it. The conveyance was just large enough for the comfortable accommodation of one person. It was moved by two tattooed coolies, one drawing and the other pushing. Coolies employed in family service wear loose sacks, which afford a more substantial covering than tattoo. The passenger is protected from rain by oiled paper covering the top of the vehicle, and enclosing the person as if in a bag. Few horses are to be seen in the streets, and they are not for hire. They belong to foreigners residing in the country. Horses are required only for long journeys. We entered a lacquer-shop, and saw many beautiful pieces of furniture, and rich bronzes with elaborate gold and silver inlaid work. This bronze-work is a specialty of the country, forming one of its chief industries. We went to the "Bluffs," a high promontory overhanging Mississippi Bay just beyond the crowded thoroughfare of the city. Here foreigners and American missionaries live. We stopped at a very attractive tea-house, and had a cup of tea, and a chat, through our interpreter, with the tea-maid. The scenery is picturesque, and the garden cultivation is perfect. We passed fields of rice where the laborers, both men and women, were almost naked, the tattooed men wearing only loin-cloths, and the women a short, scant skirt scarcely covering them from the waist to the knees. They get eight cents a day for their toil, and consider themselves fortunate in obtaining steady work. We saw evergreen trees dwarfed in all shapes, and lovely bamboo cottages with thatched roofs and small green bushes growing here and there in the thatch, and little tufts of grass cropping out under the eaves. The children of the poor, from eight to ten years of age, are entirely naked, and never have a thread of clothing on their bodies until they are about twelve years of age. A Japanese is not allowed to wear whiskers until he becomes a grandfather ; hence old bachelors may have no beard. The 'rickshaw coolies take a trotting gait and keep it as long as they go. Sometimes they make long leaps accompanied with a good-natured yell, both coolies jumping together. This movement ends with a jerk, causing an unpleasant sensation to the passenger. They get over the ground as fast as horses. An active coolie can make fifty or sixty miles a day and not feel fatigued. The waiters at our hotel are scantily clothed. They wear a loose frock coming just below the knees, but no shirt. Although their legs are bare, their stockingless feet are encased in toe slippers.

Foreigners are not permitted to take up their residence in all parts of Japanese cities, but only in certain sections set apart for their occupation. The tea-houses employ young and pretty little Japanese maids, with teeth as white as pearls and complexions as soft and peachy as powder and rouge can make them. These girls wear bright-colored loose silk sack dresses, with front *à la V.*, somewhat open. Their hair is elaborately put up with brass pins and rings. Their feet and legs are bare. They adorn themselves with many jade ornaments. The passer-by is induced to stop for a cup of tea by the winning smiles and personal attractions of the pretty tea-maids. The beauty of a Japanese girl changes as soon as she is married. She then blackens her teeth and neglects to make herself attractive, that she may indicate to her husband that she is devoted and faithful to him, and that she may be distinguished from unmarried women. Girls and boys at the age of five years begin to be nurses. The babies are strapped on the children's backs, and are thus carried about while the mother is at her work. The Japanese are fond of birds. We have seen some beautifully-colored birds, including white canaries, which seemed to be as much at home about the house as the members of the family.

Hucksters carry through the streets, in their hands, tiny stoves containing live coals, and uncooked fish and vegetables. A frying-pan is strapped to their shoulders. They cook on the sidewalks, and quickly serve the food "piping" hot to their customers. The coolies huddle around these itinerant cooks in groups, and wait their turn for a meal. The coolies neither sleep nor eat under a roof. They get their food on the street, and with a mat and a cotton sack they seek a night's shelter in some corner of a thoroughfare. A little colony of them sleep under the veranda of our hotel.

A Japanese mirror is a round plate of polished steel, with a short handle. A lady making her toilet has one held before her by her maid. The street-barber and hair-dresser in like manner hold these mirrors for their customers.

We have seen the process of firing or curing tea for exportation. In Yokohama there is one house which employs three thousand men and women during the "curing" season, and we had the good fortune to visit the place and observe the process. The men at work wore only loin-cloths, and the women short, scant skirts reaching from their waists to their knees. The tea-firers are paid twenty-five cents for ten hours' work. The firing is a simple process, and quickly done. The tea is partly sun-dried at the time of picking. In this condition it is fit for home consumption. The tea to be exported is brought from the country to Yokohama and Tokio, where there are proper facilities for curing it. It is fired in small sheet-iron pans arranged over a slow charcoal fire made of two or three live coals. A brick furnace and a pan are assigned to each person. The pan contains three pounds of tea, which must be kept constantly in motion by hand for one hour. By stirring the tea with the bare hand there is no danger of burning it, and thereby depriving the leaf of its life. The pan must be cooled immediately when it becomes too hot to be held in the hand. When cured the tea is thrown into large sieves by which the broken leaves and dust are sifted out. The tea is then placed in large bins, and when sufficiently cooled and flavored is ready for packing. The dust of the dried tea-leaves is sent to the United States and to other markets, where it is used for "doctoring" wines and liquors. In Japan there is but one kind of tea grown, although there are several grades of it. The choicest qualities are not exported, but are kept for home consumption in the families of the wealthy. Tea of good quality can be bought at prices varying from ten to sixty cents a pound, but the best tea is sold for ten dollars a pound. This high-priced tea is flavored with the tea-blossom, and the leaf is carefully prepared by hand.

Another large industry of Japan is the manufacture of lacquer-ware, in which the Japanese excel the world. Lacquer-ware is made mostly for exportation. I have been in several Japanese houses, and the only lacquer-work which I have seen in them was a little cabinet for *curios*. The lacquer is a thick liquid obtained from trees, which are tapped at certain seasons of the year. It is of a resinous nature and of a light color. It is reduced to the proper consistency by evaporation, and is afterward colored. This peculiar varnish is susceptible of a very high polish, and endures a long time. In some of the temples we have seen lacquered flooring in front of the idols, and in one we were told that the floor on which we were walking had been used a hundred years, The lacquer was quite fresh in color and but little indented by use. Foreigners cannot bear the unwholesome odors arising from the manufacture of the varnish. A great variety of lacquer-work is offered for sale in all districts frequented by strangers. There is a large exportation of it to foreign countries. Age improves the lacquer-work. In the manufacture of bronze the Japanese greatly excel. They make the finest bronze known to-day. They have the art of inlaying gold, silver, and ivory in their best bronze productions, thereby largely enhancing the beauty and increasing the cost of them. The finest bronze is of a light iron color. I have seen a pair of small vases the price of which was $1,500, and they could not be bought for less. Some of the costly bronzes now find their way out of the country, but in earlier days only the daimios or princes possessed the best which were made.

On one of our détours we visited the famous Temple of Diabutsu. The description given us of this mammoth idol by a Buddhist priest in attendance, and who acted as guide, is the following: Diabutsu, the colossal bronze idol at Kamakura, is fifty feet high and of corresponding circumference. The face is eight and a half feet long, the eyes are three and a half feet wide, the ears six feet long, the mouth three feet wide and the nose four feet long. One thumb, standing upright, is three and a half feet in circumference. The knees are twenty-four feet in circumference. The figure is that of a man in a sitting position, with the legs turned under the body *à la Turque.* Respecting the correctness of the proportions of the figure I cannot vouch. Four of our party stood in the palm of the hand of the gigantic idol. In constructing it three hundred tons of the finest bronze were used. Diabutsu is one hundred and fifty years old, and is considered one of the most sacred idols in the country. Near by Diabutsu we saw another idol, made of gilded wood. It is forty-three feet high, and represents a man in a standing position. It was, as we were informed, erected

one thousand two hundred years ago. An old woman acted as our guide. She blessed us for the fee of a few *cash*, or coppers, we gave her, by rubbing her hands on the feet of the idol, and then placed the palms on our foreheads. We went a little farther in the interior and visited the Shinto Temple filled with rich idols having numerous offerings on their necks, such as strings of *cash* and long silk ribbons on the ends of which prayers are printed. Near the temple is a large brown inclosed stone, shaded by a japonica tree. The stone is worshiped by disappointed women, and by men and women in search of their affinities, or eligible mates in marriage.

CHINA.

SHANGHAI, CHINA, October 18. Shanghai is enclosed by a high wall, four miles in circumference. The city has a population of five hundred thousand. No foreigner is allowed to reside within its walls. Foreigners occupy the "concession grounds" outside the city. In the concession a large number of residents are engaged in various pursuits of trade and commerce. The streets of the city are about ten feet wide, and are paved with large square stones. These narrow thoroughfares are very dirty and full of disgusting sights and smells. There are no sidewalks. The houses on the principal streets are used for shops. There are no windows on the first floors of the buildings; the entire front is open during the day, and closed by heavy lattice-work at night. The merchant lives in the second story, which is only a loft, or rough shelter for the family. Streets are shaded by large oiled-paper signs suspended from the upper part of the houses and extended across the thoroughfares. These signs enumerate the articles for sale, with their prices, and the particular inducements offered by the different shop-keepers. The streets are filled with idlers. The only conveyances are sedan-chairs carried by coolies. In the European concession small ponies are employed for transportation. The vehicles used are called "traps," a name borrowed from the English. The favorite conveyance in Shanghai is a wheelbarrow, with the wheel in its center and on each side of it a seat. The vehicle is wheeled by a coolie. We have ridden in many kinds of carriages, but never until now on a wheelbarrow. There is no particular quarter in which the rich merchants live. Their houses are interspersed with those of the poor, and they live over their own shops in a very humble way. Endeavoring to conceal their riches, they often bury their money in the ground in some spot known only to themselves. If they did not do this, a large part of their property would be demanded for tribute. When a rich Chinaman is "tracked" by the Government, and his possessions discovered, the greater part of his wealth is appropriated by it. We have driven on the "Bubbling Well Road," which derives its name from the boiling spring three miles from the city, in the concession district. The road is macadamized and is as smooth as a floor. There are many beautiful villas along the road which are occupied by foreigners.

A novel sight to us is that of men carrying fans, which they use for sunshades when desirable. When the fan is not in use it is placed at the back of the neck, under the blouse, with one end projecting beyond the right ear. The Chinamen know how to use the fan quite as coquettishly as do our ladies at home. We do not see many women in the streets. Now and then a sedan-chair goes by with the curtains drawn down, causing us to imagine a woman is secluded within.

The junks in the harbor are alive with women and children who seem to be scarcely two removes from the progenitors of Man, judging by the Darwin theory. These boat-women wear the merest apology for a dress. Their feet grow to the natural size. Only the higher class of women have cramped and distorted feet, causing them to walk with great difficulty; the binding of the feet causes a gait similar to walking on stilts. The social status of a Chinese woman is determined somewhat by the size of her feet. If they have been bound up and cramped at an early age they indicate that the woman is of high degree, and has never been compelled to perform any manual labor. The women destined to be children's nurses have feet about half the natural length, and walk with an unsteady gait. The Chinese have not the attractive faces and manners of the Japanese. The Japanese look jolly and coquettish, while the Chinaman seems never to smile.

In Shanghai the punishment for stealing is cruelly severe. Your father was present the other day at the trial of a Chinaman for stealing a few *cash*. The man was found guilty, and sentenced to receive two hundred blows. The punishment was at once administered. He was stripped bare and laid upon the floor. A stout man gave him fifty blows on the back and legs with a heavy piece of bamboo. A second whipper gave him fifty more, and finally the fourth finished the two hundred. The man did not utter a groan until the last fifty blows were commenced. Then the judge cried out, "Harder! harder!" When all the blows had been inflicted, the criminal's bleeding and swollen flesh was dressed with salt and water. Then he was ordered to leave the place. The only recourse for this suffering and bleeding human being was to go into the streets and beg his living, or to lie down and die of starvation.

CANTON, October 31. The scenery along Pearl River is tame and uninteresting, save that of the rice-fields, banana-groves, pagodas, and a luxuriant growth of cacti. The shores are flat. We approached Canton through a fleet of junks alive with women and children. Thousands of human beings annually born on the craft in the river spend their lives on the water and never go ashore. Generation after generation live in these floating homes, and never know any other. If a junk becomes overpopulated with children, the ordinary precautions for preventing their crawling overboard and dropping into the river are not exercised. When one of the little undesirable innocents falls into the stream and is drowned, it is deemed to be the will of the Higher Power, and the mother is comforted by the thought. More care is taken of infant boys than of infant girls. Boys are more useful than girls. If a Chinaman having two boys

A CHINESE JUNK.

and two girls is asked how many children he has, he will answer two children and two "piecee girl." The idea sought to be conveyed is that boys are worthy to be called children, and that "piecee girl" designates the inferiority of girls. So if feminine babies are too abundant, it is not a difficult matter to arrange that more boys than girls shall continue to be members of the family circle. The daily life of this boat population is always in view. When the concert and theatre junks, brilliantly lighted with lanterns, take convenient positions, the people on the smaller junks propel their craft close to them to witness the plays and to hear the music. When a girl is married and taken to another boat with her trousseau, consisting of a change of dress and a rice-kettle, she perhaps will never leave it, except to visit her friends. On the gayly flag-decorated junks, illuminated by brightly-colored lanterns and enlivened by the music of the tam-tam, girls half-dressed or dressed only for exposition are to be seen moving merrily about, and inviting their "cousins" to come on board to visit them.

Canton has a population of one million, including the river people. The Chinese wage a civil war in a very convenient manner. Whatever may be the question of the war, when the chow-chow gongs are beaten the combatants on both sides at once suspend hostilities and appease their hunger. When the meal is finished, the fight is resumed. Such struggles are commonly settled by a committee from the Feng-Shui, which is remunerated by the gift of some *cash* from both parties.

Chinese servants wind their long braids of hair around their heads when engaged at their work, but as a mark of respect when they come before their superiors let them down.

The Chinese have not as fine taste in coloring or in inventing as the Japanese. They value the jade-stone above every other precious stone. Chinese officials in high places wear a ring of white or green jade on the thumb.

I have learned in Canton to distinguish between a fine and a poor quality of tea. We are served with tea for which twenty dollars a pound was paid. The high price of the fine teas is owing to the fact that only the last leaves which open on a plant are used. They are carefully picked so that the larger leaves on the lower part of the plant may not be injured, which are picked later, when they are larger grown and stronger and of a ranker flavor. A plant yields only a few delicate leaves, and to obtain a small quantity of them a large field must be harvested. These leaves are sun-dried. After they have been cured they are flavored with the tea-blossom. The tea is put in loose packages so that the leaves may not be compressed and their tender folds broken. When the tea is thus prepared, and is not subjected to a long sea passage, it is quite a different article from the tea we obtain at home.

We visited a joss-house and were shown the appointments of a Chinaman's Elysium. We saw several Celestials lying in bunks with countenances as blissful as if the devotees had never known anything but infantile happiness. With dull, glassy eyes and sickly smiles they saluted us as we passed them. The odors of the small and close chambers were so disgustingly disagreeable that we did not tarry long in the building. We saw a white marble pagoda with several tiers of gilded bells hanging around the outside. It was richly ornamented within with carved ivory and jade idols, and a large gilded dragon on which was mounted the principal idol. A flour mill operated by buffaloes, a silk-manufactory, and glass-blowing attracted our attention a part of the time. We were also interested by a magician apparently creating birds out of nothing and seemingly breathing life into them. Our attention was drawn to the Temple of Longevity, where liberal devotees are promised long life, and we inspected a Chinese crematory. We saw twelve fat hogs in a temple, where they are kept as sacred animals. The novelty was also enjoyed of driving a few miles along the top of the wall surrounding Canton, and we met a wedding procession in one of the streets. It was at least a half-mile long. The bride, in spangled and brightly colored attire, preceded the procession in a richly ornamented sedan-chair; a veil fringed with seed pearls hung over her face. Pagodas with tinkling gilded bells, sedan-chairs containing large and small boxes of goods, and others filled with pieces of red cotton cloth and bright-colored silks, were carried by coolies. There were idols covered with gilt and jade jewelry, a company of little boys in fantastic dresses beating gongs and tam-tams; effigies of animals ornamented with gilt and red paper figures, and at the rear of the procession were the friends of the families. Altogether it was a motley train. The bridegroom was not in the procession. He awaited at his own or his father's house for the bride, whom he had not yet seen, although bound to accept, as she has been selected according to the decree of the Feng-Shui. The principal test of the bridegroom's satisfaction is his admiration of the bride's feet. If they be too large to accord with his ideas of beauty and gentility he is disappointed, and he does not conceal his unhappiness. Small feet do not affect marriages among the lower classes, for the women belonging to them must work, while those of the higher classes are only considered to be household ornaments.

There are no street-lights in Canton. Lanterns are carried by everybody going out in the evening; if without a lantern one is liable to arrest.

Oyster shells are made available for temple windows. The insides of the shells are ground off and made almost as transparent as glass. They admit a soft and agreeable light. The vegetables here are not as savory as ours; their fibre is coarse and their substance more watery. There is a great variety of good fruit, such as I have never before seen. One of the popular courses for dinner is called "Bombay duck." It is a small, strong fish, salted and dried, and served with curried rice, boiled eggs, and cheese. It might not be an appetizing dish at home, but here it is. There is one article of food which we would not dare to order, unless upon the condition that it should be *à l' Européan*, and that is eggs. A Chinaman requires eggs to be buried six months in the ground before he will eat them.

One day we dined with the United States Consul, Colonel L. He lives in the only desirable district in Canton for the residence of a foreigner, excepting the Island of Shamien, which is just opposite it across the river. Standing by the window overlooking the river, I saw a little wooden box containing a naked infant floating down the stream. I cried, "Why does not some one save that child?" The answer came, "Oh, it is only some 'piecee girl,' who was not wanted in the family, and she has been committed to the river to meet her fate." Although infanticide is a violation of Chinese law, it is rarely if ever punished. Practically, it is no crime to let a baby drown if it fall overboard from a junk or a boat. No doubt the mother hopes by chance it may be saved from such a fate.

Our host served us at dinner with bird's-nest soup, one of the most costly luxuries to be had in Canton; costly because of the difficulty in procuring the nests. They are found on precipitous rocks overhanging the sea, and are obtained at no little risk of life. This so-called delicacy is therefore rare. One nest must suffice for the course. I did not find the soup palatable enough to make me desire any one to hazard his life for a bird's nest for a table of mine. The nest is prepared by soaking it in water, and carefully separating the cream-colored glutinous substance from the feathers, straw and leaves composing the nest, which is cut in small pieces and boiled in beef or chicken soup stock. The substance is tough and tasteless.

A description of the house and garden of a rich Chinese

official may not be uninteresting. They are surrounded by a high wall. A small door in the wall is the only entrance to the grounds. We were conducted to a large hall opening into a court-yard. From the ceiling of the hall were suspended several large and handsome Chinese lanterns. The host came to meet us and invited us to a pavilion, and requested us to take seats on a raised dais, covered with red cloth, he taking a lower seat. Here tea and pipes of tobacco were served us by the servants, who were in holiday dress. After an interpreted chat, a walk in the garden followed. We were pleased to inspect the beautiful fountains containing gold-fish, the profusion of flowers, the rare trees, the exquisite plants, exotic with us, and the grottoes and caverns connected by subterranean passages lighted with Chinese lanterns. In the grottoes were a number of strange idols and some marble tablets inscribed with wise sayings. On the summit of an artificial rock, sixty feet high, was a pavilion decorated with gorgeous lanterns and containing some choice specimens of porcelain and bronzes. Here we saw dwarfed forest trees, variously shaped, with tiny leaves. There was one trained in the form of a Chinese junk; another shaped like a pagoda, with little gilded bells hanging from the branches, and another like a dragon, with glass eyes. There were several formed as bird-cages, in one of which were birds that appeared perfectly at home in their foliage-embowered cages. Another tree shaped as a man had a china plate on which the facial features were painted. The hands and feet were represented on other plates. Many other curious devices on the growing trees were shown us. The trees bore very small white blossoms, having three tiny petals. We did not have the opportunity of dining in this house. A grand Chinese dinner, as we are informed, is one of considerable formality. Etiquette requires that each guest must endeavor to persuade the one next him at table to be seated first. After some complimentary deference and hesitation on the part of the guests, they all sit down simultaneously. The dinner begins with sweetmeats and condiments, each guest helping himself with chop-sticks from the dishes passed around. There are no plates on the table. Then comes a course of dried melon-seeds, the host serving them by the handful, and with them hot wine made from rice. Bird's-nest soup follows, which is drunk from cups. No beef or mutton is used by the Chinese, because Confucius said that it was not proper to take the life of an animal useful in agriculture. Pork, ham, fish and pigeon eggs form the chief part of the dinner. The host to honor a guest selects some choice morsel and conveys it to him on his chop-sticks. The delicate attention must on no account be refused. Bowls of rice form the last course. Occasionally between the courses tobacco-pipes are passed. Cups of choice tea are then served. The honored guest is conducted to his sedan-chair, and the host shaking his own hands bids him good-bye. A dinner may continue three or four hours. Chinese women never appear in the presence of foreigners. They are secluded and treated as inferiors; even those among the higher class are thus treated.

The streets in Canton have some very significant names, such as the following, which, translated into English, mean Longevity, Benevolence, Everlasting Love, One Thousand Grand-sons, Accumulated Blessings, Reposing Dragons, Refreshing Breezes. The shops are also strangely named. One is designated Never Ending Success, another Heavenly Happiness, another Honest Gains, and another By Heaven Much Prospers. We passed by many eating-houses where cats and rats were included in the fare, and the dressed animals were suspended at the doors of the restaurants to attract attention. Eggs whose shells were "black and blue" with age were exposed among the edibles.

NATIVES OF SINGAPORE.

SINGAPORE.

SINGAPORE, November 11. We arrived here this afternoon and are seventy-five miles north of the equator. Here the days and nights are of equal duration. The sky is seldom clear. Every day there is more or less rain falling. The sun heats the moist air and makes it disagreeably vaporous. There is much lightning but little thunder in this locality. Fruits and vegetables are always growing and maturing. Indigenous fruits form a large part of the food of the people, and the sea furnishes fish in abundance, hence it is no wonder the natives are indolent. Why should they toil? They require little or no clothing, and only bamboo huts in which to sleep.

Singapore is an island twenty-four miles long and fourteen wide. It is situated in the Straits of Malacca. It is a British province ruled by native princes acknowledging allegiance to the English crown. It has a mixed population of one hundred thousand, including fifty thousand Chinamen, ten thousand Malays, five thousand Europeans and a few Americans. Here we ride in *gharries*, a little box of a wagon drawn by two small ponies. The Malay coolies wear a little more clothing than the Japanese do. Besides the red loin-cloths, they have narrow strips of white cotton cloth hanging over their left shoulders.

Our hotel comprises several buildings two stories high connected by covered corridors. It is well shaded by large trees and picturesquely environed by ornamental shrubbery and flowering plants. The wide verandas are furnished with bamboo chairs, settees and little tables where one may have a refreshing beverage or a cup of tea. In the trees flit richly-plumed birds, and among the bushes and flowers are many bright-winged butterflies. In the rooms and on the verandas are unnumbered insects, the pests of the tropics, which partly rob one of pleasure and repose. In the same inclosure with the hotel the Stars and Stripes designate the residence of the American Consul. The only native women seen on the streets are those of the lower classes. There is very little distinguishable difference in the men's and women's dress among the natives. Both wear bracelets either of jade, silver, or some cheaper metal, and ear-rings and nose-rings of gold or silver. The men have a proud bearing. They tread the ground with an independent air as if they owned it. Evidently the women are the meeker sex.

Formerly there were many tigers on the island, and until recently an average of three persons were killed weekly by them. Of late they have been vigorously hunted and large numbers are slain every year. Monkeys, parrots and other birds are carried about the streets by hucksters and are offered for sale at very low prices.

November 12. This morning we arose at five o'clock and after a cup of coffee went to visit the Whampoo gardens. We started in a warm rain, but in an hour the sky was clear. Mr. (Ah) Whampoo, a rich Chinaman, cordially welcomes strangers who go to visit his gardens. He speaks English fluently. The grounds comprise an area of fifty acres, all under fine cultivation. Here Chinese gardening may be seen in perfection. Its marked feature is dwarfing trees in an infinite variety of shapes. A certain evergreen is best suited for this purpose. The tree has a small leaf like the box of our gardens, and a tiny white flower not much larger than the head of a pin. These gardens contain every kind and color of tropical vegetation in the highest state of perfection, and also many trees and plants from different parts of the world. Ah Whampoo called our attention to some evergreens, flowering shrubs, and fruit trees which had

THE ENTRANCE TO THE WAMPOO GARDENS, SINGAPORE.

been sent him from America. We saw the Victoria lily here in its perfect beauty. The leaf of the plant is dark green veined with brown and red; it is from eight to ten inches in diameter, with its edge turned up about two inches deep all round. The flower is a pinkish white and lies partly on the leaf of the plant and partly in the water. Each plant has one leaf and one flower. The lily is called "La Belle." We saw some rare orchids and many varieties of cacti with white, red, yellow and green flowers. We saw a dwarfed growing evergreen shaped like a coupé standing about three feet high and a horse attached. We also saw other trees growing in the shape of pagodas, dogs, birds, men and women, and many other curious forms of tree growth. These trees are in full blossom now. Chinese gardeners might become interesting novel writers, for they certainly express much sentiment in the attractive forms of ornamental trees. There were also in the gardens cocoanut, nutmeg, and cinnamon trees, besides the tea, coffee, and clove plants, and an interesting menagerie of animals, fish, and birds.

In Singapore the European women wear white muslin dresses; the gentlemen wear white linen. The Singalese, on the contrary, exhibit their shiny, iron-colored bodies and jewelry in lieu of any adornment of clothing.

CEYLON.

POINT DE GALLE, November 18. Point de Galle has a population of fifty thousand, of whom the greater number are Malays and Chinese. There are but few shops here; goods and wares are sold on the verandas of the hotels and in little temporary booths erected near them. Gold sovereigns are in demand here. The native jewelers importune the stranger at every corner to sell them the coins, which are made up into jewelry. These peripatetic merchants are Malays. They speak a little "pidgin English," and are unrelenting in their solicitations, and will follow a desired customer for days to induce him to buy something. The jewel merchants dress very well when they come to the hotels, but the traffickers in other articles wear short white linen pantaloons and long frocks of colored silk open in front to display a red waistcoat. Their costume is finished with a bright scarf thrown over the left shoulder. They generally go barefooted, but when they present themselves on the verandas they wear on their feet yellow toe-slippers. If barefooted they are seen with jeweled (Manchester glass) rings on their toes They wear finger-rings and ear-rings, often having two rings in each ear—one at the top and another at the bottom of the lobe. The ear jewels are usually uncut rubies, sapphires, and pearls. Some of these are of considerable value. The merchants comb their long, black, greased hair back from their foreheads and confine it with handsome round shell combs, such as little girls at home wear. They make salaams with smiles and compliments, whether you buy of them or not. Inasmuch as the salaams cost nothing and may bring customers, the merchants, therefore, are unsparingly polite. They offer for sale some very pretty fabrics and curious embroideries, but their principal wares are

JEWEL PEDDLERS AT POINT-DE-GALLE, ISLAND OF CEYLON.

tortoise-shell work, gold and silver jewelry, carved ivory trinkets, seed pearls, and finger-rings set with uncut rubies, sapphires and emeralds. While these dealers may have many real and beautiful gems, for they are abundant in Ceylon, they have also excellent imitations in Manchester glass which only a practiced eye can detect and for which the sellers ask the price of the real stones. If the customer detects the counterfeit, the merchant politely explains that a mistake had been made in the price marked. The jewel venders frequent the hotels the day long and greatly annoy travelers. They solicit one by saying, "Buy this, please, just to start some luck." If you buy a trinket to get rid of one of them, you are likely to be just as much importuned the next day by the same person. Fine gems are found in Ceylon, but American and European jewelers have agents here to buy them as soon as they are offered for sale, and hence it is that only the less perfect ones are usually trafficked on the hotel verandas. Sometimes it may happen, however, that really beautiful and valuable gems can be obtained from these merchants.

We have strolled the streets, where many novelties have interested us. The natives show more fondness for jewelry than for clothing. Both men and women are bejeweled from their heads to their feet, while their bodies are only covered with a scant skirt of thin muslin. All have their right shoulders and breasts exposed. The children, until they reach the age of ten years, are as nude as when they were born, if the bracelets and anklets of glass or iron, and the bands of silver around their bodies with tinkling little bells attached, are excepted. If too poor to possess silver bands, they have red ribbons encircling their bodies. The poorer people chew betel-nuts, which blacken the teeth and thereby make their expression repulsive. They know nothing of table etiquette, but eat in common from a large wooden bowl. There are many cocoanut trees growing in different parts of the city, and forests of cocoanut and cinnamon trees in the suburbs. The cocoanut tree attains a height from fifty to eighty feet; not a knot or a branch is visible except at the very top, where the fruit is seen beneath a tuft of leaves. A tree commonly bears a dozen nuts. The coolies who climb the trees to get the nuts are given one for the picking of the fruit on each tree. Fresh cocoanuts are largely used for food among the natives. The milk, before the meat has thickened, is deliciously cool and very refreshing. To enjoy a cocoanut one should obtain it at this stage of its growth. The milk is then of the consistency and color of cream, and is eaten with a spoon. We have seen acres of ground covered with split cocoanuts, which were exposed to the heat of the sun in order to obtain the oil. The fibre of the shell of the cocoanut is utilized in the manufacture of rope, mats, and canvass.

I can now understand why such hot sauces as curry, chutney, onion and red pepper are so universally used in these tropical climates. They stimulate the appetite and give tone to the stomach. The use of quinine is a necessity until one becomes somewhat acclimated.

EGYPT.

CAIRO, January 26. Now we are in the land of the Pharaohs. We arrived in Cairo on the 10th inst. From Bombay to Suez is a voyage of three thousand miles. We feel that we are again in the land of European civilization. From Suez, where we left the steamer, to this city is a journey of nine hours. The road passes through an edge of the Great Sahara Desert, running for many miles over the sandy plain. We had in sight long stretches of the Suez Canal. We ran along for miles in the valley of the Nile. This is a rich and fertile tract of land, which in comparison with the desert looks like ribbons of green laid down upon either side of the river.

I have had the pleasure of making a visit to the Khedive's harem, where I went upon invitation of the Princess Mansoor, the eldest daughter of the Khedive by his first wife, and the only wife of Pasha Mansoor. The princess very graciously received us—the wife of the American Consul and myself. She speaks French and we were able to converse with her. A lady of honour attended her. We were met at the entrance of the palace garden by four handsome young Circassian slaves beautifully attired in bright, long-trained silk dresses, wearing jaunty, gayly colored silk turbans, satin slippers, and rich jewelry. They grasped our hands, and conducted us, each of us walking between two slaves, to the door of the palace, where we were received by two Nubians, male slaves, dressed in rich broadcloth, and four slave girls beautifully arrayed in many colors. The girls laid aside our wraps and then conducted us through a long and wide corridor and up a magnificent marble staircase, a girl on each side of us, who almost lifted us up the stairs as if to spare us the effort of walking.

We were shown into a large and richly furnished waiting-room, where we were received by the princess's lady of honor, and offered chibouks and coffee. The stems of the chibouks were about six feet long, with mouth-pieces of amber and bowls of gold, and were covered with gold and silver filagree work. The mouth-pieces were encircled with diamonds, rubies and emeralds. Silver plates were placed upon the floor at convenient distances to rest the bowls upon. We admired the beautiful pipes, and regretted for the moment that American ladies had not acquired the habit of smoking tobacco. Coffee was served *á la Turque*, in cup-holders studded with diamonds, which won our admiration.

Very soon six more pretty slaves, beautifully dressed and richly jeweled, came to announce that the princess would receive us. After passing through several magnificent rooms, followed by the train of girls, we reached the door of the grand salon where the princess, surrounded by a bevy of still more richly-attired slaves, advanced to meet us and led the way to a large and luxurious divan, on which we seated ourselves. Chibouks were brought to us again; we held ours in our hands while the princess made a graceful use of hers. She kindly accepted our regrets for abstaining from smoking, and said that she was really sorry we could not enjoy what to her was a great pleasure. The tobacco was so highly perfumed that the tobacco odor was entirely destroyed. Coffee was again served. Afterward the princess was handed a box on a golden salver, from which she took a jeweled cigarette holder, and having placed in it a cigarette from a dainty little gold and silver tree standing upon an ivory table near the divan, smoked the cigarette as enjoyably as she had the chibouk. The salon was splendidly furnished and ornamented. The only picture in it was a life-size portrait of the Khedive.

After chatting pleasantly for a half hour, the princess, having taken each by the hand and walking between us, conducted us to her beautiful boudoir. She called our attention to the arrangement of its furniture, entirely Oriental in style, which she said she had designed. It was indeed elegant, with its fine mirrors and antique furniture, partly covered with rich Persian fabrics embroidered with gold and silver. Baskets and mounds of artificial flowers were tastefully disposed about the room. All the floral decorations in the palace were of the finest French artificial flowers. She then led us into her study, a real bijou of a room. Its walls were faced with mirrors, and the ceiling was elaborately gilded, light being admitted from the ceiling through stained glass, for there were no windows in the room. In the center of the room was a luxurious divan, covered with crimson velvet embroidered with gold, and pillows of the same material. Near the divan was a gold and ivory table, on which were a chibouk and a golden tobacco box. On another ivory table near it was a large salver of silver and gold, on which were a basin and ewer. It was the princess's toilet table. Near at hand was a towel of white silk embroidered with gold and silver, and a vase of Bohemian glass containing perfumed water. There were also ornaments of gold, silver and alabaster in the room.

The princess took us each by the hand again and conducted us to another beautiful room in which we were served with a delicious cordial in golden cups, with napkins embroidered with gold thread. Here the princess gracefully thanked us for the visit, and retired to her boudoir, followed by the attendants who had accompanied us through the palace. We descended the staircase, supported on either side by the same girls who had escorted us up the stairs, and were conducted to our carriage.

There were twenty-five slaves in attendance during our visit of two and a half hours. The princess has fifty Circassian slaves at her command. Everywhere we went in the palace the air was perfumed. The princess was more simply dressed than her women. She wore a plain but elegant dress of brown silk with trimmings and ornaments of tortoise-shell elaborately carved, having on them a crown and the letter "I." This letter is found on all royal emblems, it being the initial letter of the Khedive's name, "Ismail." Princess Mansoor is a handsome blonde Circassian with bright red hair. Her lady of honor is a French woman, a brunette, whose hair is dyed red to please the princess. The princess's mother is a beautiful blonde, who is even handsomer than her daughter.

The Gezeereh palace is the finest of all the palaces in Cairo. It is the palace in which royal or distinguished guests are lodged. The Khedive occupies a luxurious bungalow in the palace garden when there are guests at Gezeereh. The Prince of Wales was entertained there on his way to India. Empress Eugenie also occupied it at the time of the opening of the Suez Canal. In it is a suite of four magnificent rooms connected with an alabaster bath-room. These chambers are tapestried with blue satin and gilt trimmings. The ceilings are canopied with the same materials. Their decorations, as well as the toilet porcelain ware, are blue and gilt. There are also beautiful ornaments and pieces of furniture made of alabaster. In the salon are two large Sevres vases on which are painted the portraits of the French emperor and empress. The lunch-room, although not large, is finely proportioned. In each corner of it is an alabaster fountain, which, when notable guests are entertained, spouts perfumed water. The tables in it are of alabaster, and the draperies are of blue satin. The salons are resplendent in their crimson and white velvet and gold-embroidered white satin hangings and upholstering. In one of them are two alabaster mantels inlaid with rare stones supporting mirrors reaching to the ceiling, which are framed in inlaid alabaster. The staircase is another attractive work of art. It is of white marble and inlaid with choice stones forming antique designs.

THE EXTERIOR OF THE PAVILION OF THE PALACE OF GEZEEREH, CAIRO.

There is an exquisite marble kiosk at one end of the veranda of the palace in which there is a pretty breakfast room. The room is lined with mirrors and trimmed with artificial flowers. In each corner are exquisite little alabaster fountains from which flows perfumed water. The palace is surrounded by beautiful gardens, containing several fountains and some fine old shade trees.

There is also the Shoobra palace, about an hour's ride from Gezeereh, another wonder of Oriental architecture and splendor. The avenue leading to the palace is three miles long, and is bordered on both sides with acacia and sycamore trees. It is the fashionable drive. There every afternoon may be seen the finest turnouts of the foreign residents, the Khedive's magnificent carriages, drawn by Arabian horses with outriders in uniforms and decorations of blue and silver, crimson and gold, scores of donkeys in gilded trappings carrying Arab women closely veiled and riding astride. We also observed on this highway long trains of camels laden with stone and produce, and now and then dromedaries gayly caparisoned bearing riders in bright Oriental costumes. Such a medley of curious street scenes cannot be found in any other part of the world.

The palace is surrounded by beautiful gardens in which are scores of orange and lemon trees bending under their burdens of fruit. We had permission to pick some oranges, which were delicious. The blood or red orange grows here in perfection. We could not see the interior of the palace, but we did see the kiosk and alabaster bath. The kiosk is three hundred feet square with an artificial lake in the center, from the midst of which rises a pavilion large enough to seat thirty persons. In it are divans, cushions, plants, lamps with magnificent glass shades, and a fountain of perfumed water. The pavilion is reached by a little gondola. The lake is encircled by a marble water-course upon which are sculptured fish, reptiles, aquatic birds and animals. In each corner of the kiosk are small boudoirs where the women of the harem sip their coffee from tiny ornamented cups. These rooms are upholstered with richly-colored silks and velvets. One of these boudoirs is most elegantly furnished, it having been fitted for the viceroy, Mohammed Ali. The corridors around the lake are supported by alabaster columns, and furnished with fine mirrors and luxurious divans. They are lighted by gas. The bath is a large room faced with alabaster; the bathing basin is also of alabaster. When in use the fountain emits perfumed water. There are several small luxurious coffee-rooms adjacent to the bath-room.

The pyramids are the wonder of the world and the pride of Egypt. The group of the largest, three in all, is six miles from Cairo. The sandy road is bordered with beautiful trees, including many of the date palm, which afforded a grateful shade. On our way to the pyramids we passed the Khedive's new palace, which when finished will be one of the largest and one of the most magnificent in existence. The grounds are inclosed by fourteen miles of stone wall, ten feet high, and have a frontage on the Nile of three and a half miles. There is a group of three palaces connected by corridors already finished, and others are building. A large reservoir provided with a steam pump supplies water for the buildings and grounds. And we also passed by two imposing buildings belonging to the Khedive's sons.

As we approached the pyramids they seemed to diminish in size, as did Mont Blanc when we came near its base. The pyramids are three immense piles of masonry. The largest is the pyramid of Cheops. The great pyramid, or Cheops, is supposed to have been built about three thousand five hundred years B. C., and the smaller ones subsequently. It took ten years to build the causeway on which the stones were brought from the quarries along the Nile. It is said that one hundred thousand men were twenty years building Cheops. Each of its sides immedi-

THE PYRAMID OF CHEOPS, THE SPHYNX AND TEMPLE OF CHAFRA, CAIRO.

ately above the sand measures seven hundred and sixty feet in width, but below the sand its base must be of much larger dimensions. I do not know that excavations to the foundation of the pyramid have ever been made.

Cheops is 480 feet high. The highest structure in Europe is the tower of the Strasburg Cathedral, the altitude of which is 461 feet. St. Peter's at Rome is 429 feet high, and St. Paul's in London 404 feet.

The wonderful Sphinx stands a quarter of a mile from the great pyramid. The face of the Sphinx bears a striking resemblance to George Washington's face as pictured.

We have seen the great citadel at Cairo and the wonderful alabaster mosque. If the latter is not the largest, it is by far the richest mosque in the world. The mosque of St. Sophia in Constantinople is larger, but not so beautiful. These two buildings stand upon a rocky eminence, six hundred feet above the city, this particular location having been chosen, it is alleged, because meat would keep sweet much longer upon this high rocky ground than in any other part of the city. Saladin built the citadel in 1100. . The mosque is a modern structure. It was built by Mohammed Ali, the grandfather of the present Khedive, and who has left many magnificent monuments to mark his reign in Egypt. It is three hundred feet square. Its outside, not yet completed, will be faced with blocks of alabaster, as is the interior. The alabaster used in the construction of these buildings is a richly-colored stone, hard as granite, and of a very fine grain, with layers of amber and wavy cream-colored lines running through it. This alabaster takes a high polish and looks like satin. The architecture of the mosque is Oriental. Its roof is supported by alabaster columns. Costly Turkish carpets cover the floor. The alabaster galleries are fully fifty feet above the floor. The mosque is lighted by three rows of stained-glass windows, and in it are hundreds of hanging-glass lamps arranged in circles and triangles. Its gilded dome can be seen at a distance of twenty miles. The court leading to the mosque is paved with alabaster and is surrounded by a corridor of the same. It is the only alabaster mosque in existence.

In the palace adjoining the mosque are an elaborate staircase and a bath chamber which are marvels of beauty. Close by the river bank and not far from the citadel is a clump of bulrushes and trees occupying the spot where it is said Moses was hidden from the persecution of Pharaoh.

AUSTRIA.

VIENNA, New Year's Evening. Christmas week passed very pleasantly with us. The Christmas tree co-exists with the day in this country. Every German family must have one. The poorest will have a Christmas tree, if it be but a branch of evergreen decorated with a half-dozen wax-tapers and a gay ribbon. At the market-places, corners of the streets, and flower-shops evergreens of all sizes and at all prices may be purchased.

Here Christmas is not marked by the exchange of gifts, but is rather an occasion for a reunion of family and friends. Do not let us abandon the Christmas tree in America, even if it is a borrowed idea.

The season of social gayeties has begun, and the carnival is already under way. A carnival here is not similar to a carnival in the southern countries of Europe. The climate of the north does not permit of outdoor demonstrations ; the entertainments are indoor merry-makings, festivities, and costume and masked balls. The first court-ball will take place January 27th. Each of the ambassadors gives a grand ball during the season.

The winter climate in Vienna is by no means semi-tropical ; snow falls in considerable quantities, but it is not allowed to stay on the ground. An army of men, women, and children is set to work to sweep it into piles as soon as it falls, and hundreds of wagons are employed to carry it off.

There is a fine rink here where skating is generally indulged in. People of high rank enjoy the amusement. A few evenings ago a beautiful skating *fête* by electric light was given. Twelve pantomimic tableaux were presented on skates while the orchestra played selections of lively music. During the evening a red-painted chariot, drawn by six white horses, gayly caparisoned, repeatedly passed around the outer circle of the rink. After the tableaux dancing was beautifully executed upon skates. A platform was erected and trimmed with crimson velvet and gilt decorations for the royal family. A large and brilliantly illuminated café, with dressing-rooms, was arranged for the skaters and spectators. The price of admission was six florins, equal to $2.40. Ten thousand tickets were sold. The Viennese are accomplished skaters. Old and young enjoy alike the exhilarating exercise.

January 29. The first court-ball of the season took place in the palace last evening. About two thousand people were present. We were presented to the empress before the ball began. The Empress of Austria is a charming woman, and although she is a grand-mother, does not appear to be more than thirty years of age. It is said that the Empress Elizabeth is the handsomest reigning sovereign. In figure she is tall, graceful, and erect. She has the fresh coloring accompanying health, large expressive dark eyes, and magnificent soft brown hair. In manner she is affable and elegant. As a friend she is sympathetic and kind. The emperor has genial manners and a pleasant word for everybody. He is a hard-worker. I understand he rises at five o'clock in the morning, and by nine o'clock he has ended his audience with his ministers.

The empress is a most accomplished equestrienne. She has in her stables five hundred white horses, the greater number being carriage horses.

The empress's toilet at the ball was simple but rich and beautiful. It was a composition of pearl-colored velvet and satin with jewels of rubies and diamonds. The Crown Princess Stephanie is charming. She is twenty-two years of age, a lovely blonde with sparkling blue eyes and beautiful golden brown hair.

Her toilet was of white satin, embroidered with silver thread. Her jewels were sapphires and diamonds.

The ball-room is spacious and grand. It was brilliantly illuminated with a double row of chandeliers, one above the other, in which were burning hundreds of wax candles. At one end of the room was a dais, or elevated platform, richly upholstered with crimson velvet and gilt trimmings, which the royal family occupied. Opposite the platform was a balcony where Strauss's orchestra of fifty musicians, directed by the famous composer, played delightful music. Around the room was an elevated platform about ten feet wide, which was filled with plants in blossom and beautiful foliage, banked up fifteen feet high. The ladies' toilets were magnificent, generally of pearl, white, and delicate rose colors; these being the empress's favorite colors, the ladies observe her majesty's preference. There was a great variety and profusion of magnificent jewels displayed that evening. The young ladies observed strict simplicity in their toilets, which were generally of delicate shades of tulle, with few jewels, but lovely ribbons and flowers for ornamentation.

With so much brilliancy and beauty, combined with the music, flowers, and the flashing jewels, and, in addition, the uniforms of the diplomats of different countries, richly embroidered with gold and silver thread, the Hungarian court dress, which is composed of velvet, fur, and precious stones, and the Austrian court and military uniforms,—than which none can be more brilliant,—it was indeed a fairy scene, and one long to be remembered. Invitations to the court-balls are given for nine o'clock. The dancing begins at ten, and at a quarter of an hour before midnight, when the emperor and empress leave the ball-room, the guests depart.

February 18. The second court ball is over. It was a finer *fête* and more exclusive in invitations than the first ball. There were seven hundred and twenty guests in attendance. The grand entrée in the ball-room took place at ten o'clock, and after two rounds of dancing, supper was served. There were seventy-two tables laid in a half-dozen rooms, each table seating ten persons and presided over by some representative of royalty or nobility. The empress left the ball-room before the supper was announced and did not re-appear. Supper being over, the emperor and the Crown Princess Stephanie led the way to the ball-room when the cotillion was danced, and at twelve o'clock the royal family left the ball-room and the company immediately dispersed. The floral decorations remained the same as at the first ball. I never saw such magnificent toilets and profusion of jewels as were there displayed. The Polish, Bohemian, Croatian and Hungarian costumes of the government officials greatly enhanced the attractiveness of the spectacle. I saw ladies wearing jeweled necklaces estimated at seventy thousand dollars in value, and tiaras of diamonds exceeding that sum, besides bracelets, buckles and agraffes of great beauty and cost. The bodice of one toilet was ornamented around the points with a dozen clusters of diamonds. The empress's toilet was of cream-colored satin, embroidered with gold ; her jewels were emeralds and diamonds. The crown princess's dress was of rose satin and velvet of the same color, brocaded with gold thread ; her jewels were pearls and diamonds. Many of the family jewels of the Viennese are of almost priceless value. They are, in many cases, heirlooms and the inheritance of several generations, with additions in each decade, so that the original cost of them is not to be compared with modern prices. In olden times the diamond was not appreciated as it is in these days and had not the same value. Precious stones were then only possessed by the families of royalty and of nobility, and the demand for them was quite limited. In earlier days some of the old Austrian and Hungarian families had great possessions, and they obtained every fine gem that was merchantable in their countries. This is the explanation of the enormous collection of jewels in these countries. A very pretty and pleasing feature of the ball was the distribution of beautiful bonbonniéres to the guests when they departed from the ball-room.

This is the time of year for "coffees"—especially a German custom. They are largely in vogue with the Viennese. The fashionable hour for them is four o'clock in the afternoon, and ladies attending them always carry their work-bags. The guests are expected to arrive promptly at the hour named in the invitation. They remove their hats and wraps, and pass an hour in conversation and work until coffee is announced. The guests are seated at a table, which is prettily laid with choice china, bonbons, and flowering plants sprinkled with perfumed water. A delicious cup of coffee, *à la Viennoise*, with thin slices of buttered bread, plain cakes, fruit-jellies and fruit-creams comprise the simple repast. Sometimes there are readings, which occupy an hour very agreeably before the coffee is announced. Very soon after the refreshments have been served the ladies separate, with the parting words, *auf wiedersehen*, or *au revoir*.

HUNGARY.

BUDAPEST, May 3. We came here to attend the opening of the first Hungarian national exposition. From Vienna it is five hours' ride by rail, or twelve hours by steamer on the Danube River.

Budapest is on the Danube, and embraces the municipalities of Pest on one side and Ofen on the other side. The two cities were annexed in 1873, since which time the greater number of improvements have been made. Budapest is a city of street cafés. From early morning until midnight they are patronized. From four o'clock in the afternoon until nine in the evening they are enlivened with music. The Hungarian music is of a weird and mournful character; it is called gypsy music. It is generally in the minor key and played without notes. At our hotel we have this music daily for two hours during the time dinner is served.

The Hungarians are more stirring than the Austrians. The Hungarian language is used in social and business relations more now than formerly. Hungarians have bright and keen faces which indicate great earnestness of purpose. The exposition is the grandest affair that has taken place here since the crowning of the king and queen twenty years ago. Nobles, aristocracy and peasants are in their best attire these days.

The opening ceremony occurred yesterday in the park where the exposition is held. Crown Prince Rudolph read the opening speech in the Hungarian language. It was addressed to the king and announced the object of the exposition and its importance to the people. The king replied in a few words; he also used the Hungarian language and wished success to the enterprise. These addresses concluded, the king, with the Princess Stephanie on his arm, followed by the Hungarian and Austrian ministers, the diplomatic corps and the nobility, made the tour of the principal buildings. Opposite the royal pavilion was an elevated platform furnished with cushioned chairs for the ladies of the nobility and of the diplomatic corps.

The favorite Hungarian color is vermilion; this color is worn for gentlemen's neck ties. Several ladies of the diplomatic corps wore toilets of that color, including hats and parasols, in compliment to the occasion. All the bunting decorations of the grounds were of the same color, which made a striking and brilliant contrast with the green foliage of the trees. The Hungarian nobles wore superb costumes of velvets, furs, and gold embroideries, richly ornamented with precious stones. I observed several costumes with buttons of fine pearls, turquoises, carbuncles and emeralds set with diamonds. All the nobles wore upon their velvet or fur caps aigrettes of feathers and precious stones. I saw an aigrette of turquoise and diamonds as large as a tea saucer!

Imagine the spectacle of one hundred of these magnificent costumes and several hundred more of richly-dressed military officers moving about on the bright green grass under a forest of trees in spring verdure! There were also hundreds of ladies to be seen in brilliant toilets and sparkling with diamonds in the bright sunlight. Waving white plumes on the velvet caps of the aristocracy added not a little to the beautiful picture. The plain black suit of the American minister was not left unmentioned by the newspapers. I observed in a German journal this morning a paragraph which stated that among the different uniforms the extreme republican plainness of the American minister's dress was conspicuous.

The procession, in which there were royal personages, foreign notables, and persons of nobility, escorted by a fine display of military, passed through Andrassy Avenue to the exposition grounds. All buildings along the avenue were decorated with flags, rich tapestries, oriental fabrics, shawls, velvet draperies, and Turkish carpets suspended from the windows and balconies.

The route from Vienna to Budapest is through the valley of the Danube River, a rich agricultural country. The different grains are already well advanced in growth, and the fruit-trees are loaded with green fruit. Lilacs in this country attain a luxuriance and beauty that I have not seen elsewhere. The lilacs here are of three shades—purple, a delicate peach blossom, and a very rich cream-white color. Along the route we saw hedges of lilacs resembling ribbons of purple satin laid upon the grass.

The Hungarian peasant costume is picturesque. Women wear bright-colored short skirts, reaching just below the knees, black bodices with white sleeves, and chemisettes, high-topped boots meeting their skirts, and bright ribbons or handkerchiefs arranged jauntily upon their heads. The men wear coarse white home-spun linen trousers, nearly as wide as the women's skirts and just long enough to cover their knees, gayly colored open jackets, with bright cords dangling from the front lapels, black felt broad-brimmed hats, with a little brown or green feather stuck in the band on one side, and low shoes with large showy buckles.

The nurse-girls in Budapest, as in Vienna, are generally Croatian women, and their costume is becoming and serviceable. They wear short skirts of bright colors, generally red, with black bodices over white chemisettes and short flowing sleeves, high-topped boots, made of fine leather, with high heels; their coiffure is a large double bow, made of bright ribbon, eight or ten inches wide, having streamers extending to the bottom of their skirts. You can imagine how bright and cheerful the streets of Budapest look with these pretty costumes thronging them.

Respecting the wines of Hungary I may say that everybody knows that the delicious Tokay is made in this country, and that even the *vin ordinaire* here is excellent. There are many varieties of good wines here, to be had at low prices. In the south of Hungary the grape is a very important product.

From a high point near the palace,—Blocksberg, five miles distant—is seen the valley from which the Hunyadi bitter water is obtained. This water is exported to the United States in great quantities, and it is also extensively used in Europe.

Pest was built by the Bulgarians long before Ofen, where the palace stands, and yet Pest has the appearance of a modern town. It has been taken and destroyed several times by the Turks, and rebuilt as many times by its own people. It was almost ruined again by the terrible inundation of 1838. In Ofen is the celebrated White Church, built by St. Stephen in 1015. Pest and Ofen were incorporated into a municipality in 1873, under the name of Budapest, since which time great improvements have been made, especially in Pest, which is rapidly becoming one of the beautiful cities of Europe.

While the better class of Austrians are a handsome people, the Hungarians have stronger and more marked features. Their complexions are as dark as those of southern countries, while the Austrians are fairer, like the people of northern Europe.

The bath-house on the Margaretha Insel, not far from Budapest, is perhaps the finest public bath building in Europe. It is a stone structure, surrounded by stately old trees and beautiful shrubbery and flowers. The baths, twenty in all, are of marble. The portiéres and upholstery are of crimson velvet. Luxurious lounges and easy chairs are found in the corridors and on the verandas, inviting rest after the bath, beside charming little nooks with fountains and flowers, and a fine restaurant, which induce a longer tarry on the grounds. The building was erected by one of the nobles of Hungary and presented to Pest.

BOHEMIA.

CARLSBAD, May 24. After a week's sojourn in Pest we returned to Vienna, and arranged our affairs for a trip to Carlsbad. From Vienna to this place is a ride by rail of twelve hours. It was one of the most interesting journeys we have ever made, at home or abroad. Every mile of the way was novel to us, and the scenery very charming. Until we reached the Bohemian frontier the country was a continuity of lowland, stretching along the valley of the Danube; but it was not without many interesting features. We passed by scores of neat-looking little farmers' villages, and miles upon miles of fruit orchards. For miles along the route the fields of ripening grain to be seen in the distance looked like measureless lengths of shaded green ribbons laid upon the ground, without a fence or hedge to mar the beautiful illusion. Emerging from the valley, we entered a rough, mountainous country, with great forests of pine and many small lakes. We soon recognized the fact that we were among the mountains of Bohemia.

We saw many bands of gypsies in camp, and others moving along the route. The numerous little villages and hamlets were pictures of quiet rural scenery. These villages contain probably from thirty to forty one-story-high white-washed houses, and a church, with its spire rising above the embowering trees. A half-dozen low houses comprise a hamlet where there may be seen a small church, or perhaps a shrine instead. Each little house seemed imbedded in rose-bushes and clumps of fruit-trees. Along the railroad are many shrines containing statues of the Holy Family. Here and there in the fields, and by the way-sides of the country roads, small shrines are erected.

I should say that Bohemia produces fruit enough for all

Europe, judging from the many orchards we saw. The highways are even shaded by apple, cherry, and plum trees, which are now in full bloom. All along the railroad are orchards with not a fence about them, nor is any sign seen indicating "hands off." The fruit here is as plentiful as pine burrs are in the Adirondacks. I don't believe the nomadic Bohemian pays much for his fruit!

Bohemia is wildly picturesque and full of scenic surprises to the traveler. The constant change of scenery from mountain to valley, with high ledges of rocks suddenly appearing, and again fields of "ribbons" of grain with a little hamlet apparently interspersed here and there, makes an enchanting variety of landscape. To me it was like passing through a picture gallery with a constant change of subjects.

The women seem to do most of the farm-work. We saw only a few men in the fields. In Europe the women and children do most of the planting and cultivating, and the harvesting too, while the men are engaged in military service. The grape is grown successfully in Bohemia, and fine wines are made there.

Carlsbad is unlike any other place in the world that we have seen in all our travels. Your father became quite infatuated with the city when he first visited it, and is even more enchanted now. He is delighted with the long rambling walks over the mountains. Every one here soon becomes a mountain-ranger, for the inducement to much walking, as a part of the scheme of cure, is most successfully effected. The ascents of the high peaks are made so gradual, and the provision of frequent pavilions with comfortable seats where one may take rest, soon teaches one that walking is the thing to do. And, too, it affords the opportunity of meeting friends, for nobody stays at home. There are fifty miles of well-constructed walks traversing the mountains and valleys in the vicinity of Carlsbad, with occasionally a café where one can take rest and refreshment. One meets here with constant surprises in the way of comfortable accommodations and charming entertainments.

Carlsbad has a population of 15,000 inhabitants. It is situated in a basin encircled by mountains, and has a rapid little stream coursing through the valley. Near this stream of sweet water are several mineral springs bursting out of the ground at intervals of one hundred to two hundred feet. The water of some of these springs has a temperature of almost boiling heat, while that of the others is tepid. There are no cold mineral waters nearer than Montoni's Gessübler spring, about two hours' drive from Carlsbad. In places along the streets the pavements are quite warm from the hot waters bubbling underneath them.

The most celebrated spring, the *Sprudel*, or Bubbling Well, discharges a stream not less than five inches in diameter, which is at a boiling heat. The water is so hot that the ladies handle the mugs containing it with napkins. It can only be taken into one's mouth by sips. The Sprudel corridor is always filled with steam. The hot water of this spring has been gushing from it for hundreds of years, except at the time of the great earthquake at Lisbon in 1755, when there was a partial subsidence. However, it resumed its full force of flow in two or three days.

The Sprudel was accidentally discovered six hundred years ago on the occasion of a deer-hunt. The animal, being closely followed by some hunters, leaped from a high ledge of rocks into this boiling spring, which was hidden by the underbrush. The dead deer was found, as also was the source of the Sprudel Spring. It is said that the hunter who drove the deer off the rocks was Carl IV., hence the derivation of the name Carlsbad, or Carl IV.'s bath. The Sprudel was a resort for invalids long before the site of the town of Carlsbad was built upon. In the early days of its discovery the nobility came from far and near, and encamped near the spring in order to drink the water. Now fifty thousand people visit Carlsbad every season.

The first promenade corridor was built in 1748. In the centre of the Sprudel corridor is a Vienna orchestra of twenty musicians, who discourse fine music from six until eight o'clock in the morning, during the time prescribed for the "cures" to drink the water. It was an odd sight this morning to see thousands of people of all nationalities, each with a glass or china mug strapped over the shoulder, walking through the long corridors of the Sprudel Spring sipping the hot water, and chatting as they strolled, or sat and listened to the music while drinking the morning draught. An invalid is instructed by one of the physicians how to take the water. The doctor first diagnoses the disease, and tells the patient the quantity of water to be taken and at what intervals. For instance, your father is instructed to go fasting to the Sprudel at seven o'clock in the morning. He is to drink one cup of water, and then to stroll twenty minutes, when he is to drink another cup, and stroll again, and then drink a third cup about eight o'clock. Then we go to the Swiss bakery, and get bread, or *zwieback*, of a certain kind eaten by the "cures," which is handed to us in a pink paper bag, and we go thence to some café along the sidewalk or to a garden where coffee or tea and two boiled eggs can be obtained, which, with our unbuttered bread, makes our breakfast.

After an hour's rest everybody falls into a line and all start for a walk to the mountains. Those who are not able to walk may get a cart and donkey, the driver walking by the side of the animal, and so the invalids are enabled to keep alongside of the good walkers. People and donkeys reach the heights by shaded paths, resting every few minutes until they have arrived at the top of some high rocky cliff, where one finds a pretty summer-house and a well-conducted café. Fine views of the surrounding country are seen through the clearings made in the intercepting woods.

One o'clock is the hour for dinner, which one may take wherever one chances to be, for there are innumerable and excellent restaurants to be found about Carlsbad, with about the same bill of fare that is provided at the hotels. There is but little choice in the cuisine; it is nearly the same thing all over Carlsbad, and only embraces a plain style of cooking. In order to insure the proper food for the "cure," his doctor will give him a written list of such articles of food as he may eat. However, it matters very little what one may wish to order, for there is only the prescribed menu to be found at the hotels and restaurants. The fare is good in quality, plainly cooked, limited in variety, and ample enough in quantity. After dinner another walk or donkey ride of two hours for one's health is taken. Then the patients may go to some garden café, and enjoy an hour of fine music. At seven o'clock a supper of cold meat and bread, with tea or a prescribed wine is allowed. No butter is served to "cures," except when ordered by the physicians. At nine o'clock, the hour for retiring, a glass of cooled Sprudel, or the water of some other spring, is drank.

No exception is made even for royalty in the early morning walk and drinking the waters at the springs. The King and Queen of Holland are now in Carlsbad and go daily at seven o'clock to the spring for two or three cups of water. There are a half-dozen principal springs which vary greatly in temperature and somewhat in mineral qualities. At each spring are six or eight "dippers"—little girls, from ten to twelve years old, wearing rubber aprons—who fill the cups and return them to the drinkers. Thousands upon thousands of persons may be seen at the springs daily during the morning hours, and it is a motley crowd as they pass along in line,—the stout and the thin invalids,—all with their mugs in hand or strapped over the shoulders, for each one must wait his turn to get his cup filled. There are often two hundred people in line, or in the circle formed around the spring. As fast as the cups are filled the "cures" fall out of line and stand on one side until they have drank their portions, and others fall into their places. Sometimes I have been five minutes in line moving slowly along to get my cup filled. As my prescription only calls for one mug of water, I have a half-hour to spare, which I spend in the Sprudel corridor and listen to the music.

All along the banks of the River Tapell running through the town are attractive shops and bazars where are for sale all kinds of small wares and Bohemian glass. Among these shops is one called the "Yankee Notion Shop," where a great variety of small American wares may be found. Some of these shops are no more than eight feet wide, and just deep enough for two people to sit behind a small counter, and a narrow space for three or four shoppers in front of it. The street running along the river is called Chestnut Alley ; it is shaded by chestnut-trees a hundred years old, whose wide-reaching branches overhang many street cafés which are established under them only for summer occupation.

It is customary here to go in parties on afternoon walks, and afterwards to a garden or café, where the ladies, having with them their inevitable work-bags, devote an hour or two to embroidery or knitting, while the gentlemen indulge in a cigar, all being seated around a large table ; at half-past six o'clock the work-bags are closed and the members of the party leisurely saunter along in the middle of the streets to their respective homes. In certain thoroughfares, where the popular springs are, no carriages are allowed during the early morning hours which are devoted to taking the waters, so that the "cures" have the entire roadway for their "constitutionals." On the other streets, where the large cafés are situated, carriages are prohibited until the morning coffee has been taken.

There is but little bathing recommended in the mineral waters of Carlsbad; indeed, many people are positively forbidden to bathe in them. The especial medicinal bath recommended for nervous derangement and rheumatic complaints is the mud bath. This bath is a mixture of clay, brought from Mariensbad, and hot Sprudel water. The clay is as black as peat, and is largely composed of iron, sulphur, and salt. The facilities for furnishing the mud bath are very perfect here. A mud bath is certainly not as agreeable as one of pure water, for one has an aversion to an immersion in dirty water. However, in many cases, it is an efficacious remedy for disease Car-loads of the clay are daily brought to Carlsbad during the summer. Generally sixty pounds of the clay are mixed with hot Sprudel water, to the consistency of a thick batter, the mass having a temperature of 28° Réaumar. The patient remains twenty-five minutes in the bath. After taking it, the attendant gives the patient a clean-water bath. Not more than a half-dozen of these baths are recommended to be taken; one every alternate day.

We have become somewhat accustomed to a sight which is very novel to Americans. The erection of an opera-house is in progress on the lot adjoining our hôtel, and the brick and mortar used in constructing the building are carried to the masons by young women. They carry the hods with no evident discomfort; they ascend and descend the ladders with as much ease as men. I have noticed among them a very comely and bright-faced girl, to whom the masons are particularly gallant, for while they permit the other women to dump their own hods, there is always a mason ready to dump hers. The girls wear short gray skirts and sleeveless jackets, long red stockings and stout wooden shoes. They seem perfectly happy in their work, if I judge rightly from their frequent singing and chatting.

PORTUGAL.

CINTRA, January 5. We came here yesterday to escape the noise and annoyance of the carnival at Lisbon, in which all classes participate. Last evening we saw a really pretty carnival spectacle. About five o'clock in the afternoon a group of eight little girls, from twelve to fourteen years old, and as many country cavaliers, about twenty years of age, formed themselves in a circle in front of our hotel, with a band of country musicians. The group danced a national dance lasting nearly an hour. The major domo of the party was dressed as a warrior of the olden time, and mounted on a gayly caparisoned white horse covered to his feet with a white net. The group was escorted by four other horsemen armed with paper weapons to protect the dancers from intrusion by passers-by.

The little girls wore white dresses, pink sashes, pink slippers with lacings of pink ribbons extending to the knees, veils of silver-tissue paper attached to crowns of roses and silver paper. They carried in their belts short paper swords, and in their hands semicircular wreaths of flowers and ribbons large enough to pass over their heads. The cavaliers wore white shirts, with broad red stripes on the outer side of them, red scarfs around their waists, red handkerchiefs about their necks, and Portuguese red and blue caps. They had also wreaths in their hands. The movements and changes of the dance were directed with a whistle by the major domo, who stood at the head of his horse. There was a standard-bearer with a flag, who took an important part in the dance. The movements of the dancers were slow and well timed with the music, and graceful beyond anything I have seen even at a court ball. One of the changes was evidently a love scene, during which the cavaliers pulled from their pockets white handkerchiefs, and throwing them on the ground, dropped each upon a knee, facing their partners, the couples placing wreaths upon one another's necks and clasping hands. Then they marched away two by two, and disappeared down the road. They departed with a light dancing step timed to the music.

We visited the beautiful quinta of Mr. C., an Englishman from London, who has an income of half a million a year. He comes to Cintra every six months to stay a few weeks. The house is built after the plan of a Moorish palace. It is the finest residence in Portugal, not excepting the king's palaces. The architecture inside and outside is entirely Moorish. The building is beautiful, with its marble halls, fountains, sculptured columns and marble lattice-work. A part of the furniture is the fine collection of Indian work which was sent to London for exhibition some years ago. For one table $5,000 was paid, and all the other pieces were purchased at high prices. There are rich Persian carpets, rare curios from Japan and China, and some marble window screens from the harem of the palace in Agra, India. There is also a collection of rare books, and many works of art, bought at enormous prices. In fact everything about this place is palatial. The house is built of white marble, situated in a large cork forest, and has close to the house acres of ground laid out in gardens and orange and lemon groves. Mr. C. claims to have trees and plants from every part of the world. He employs twenty gardeners.

We have been to Mafra, an insignificant little village in which is the largest building in Portugal, an old convent built one hundred and eighty years ago. From Cintra, seventeen miles distant, this building is plainly seen. This great pile of marble and stone is 1150 feet long, 350 feet longer than the Capitol at Washington. It was built by King John V. of Portugal,

ENTRANCE OF THE MONSERRATE PALACE AND THE SQUARE OF D. PEDRO, LISBON.

who made a vow that were a son born to him he would build in the poorest part of the kingdom the largest convent ever erected. Thirteen years were spent in its erection. The building contains 866 rooms, 5,000 doors, and 9 courts. Upon the roof 10,-000 men may stand at one time. When the basilica, or chapel, was consecrated, on the king's birthday, he ordered refreshments to be given from the kitchen to all who applied, and 9,000 persons partook of his hospitality that day. In the convent is a library of 30,000 books.

Cintra is a picturesque, rambling little town, apparently dropped down upon the eastern slope of the *serra*, or mountain, nestling among vine-covered trees, lovely gardens and orange groves. It overlooks a plain between the mountain and the sea five miles in width, dotted with twenty-three little villages and scores of vineyards, and includes a fine view of the Atlantic ocean.

The steamers passing the mouth of the Tagus are plainly seen from any part of the village. Cintra has a population of four thousand. It is the only convenient Sunday retreat for the Lisbonese ; it is distant seventeen miles over a fine road with the sea in view nearly all the way. It is made by rail in an hour. The village is built upon over-hanging cragged rocks and terraced plateaus seemingly clinging to the sides of the mountains. The seaward slope of the serra is laid out in quintas, or spacious gardens, in which stand long-ago-built villas, and there are frequent thickets of fine old forest trees overhung with moss, ivy, and flowering vines, interspersed with small groves of lemons and wild oranges. Through these quintas are narrow donkey-paths leading all over the mountains, where one is sure to meet, any day in the week, several parties of excursionists mounted on well-trained donkeys. The principal highways are bordered with stone walls six to eight feet high, many of which were built more than two hundred years ago. In many places these walls are entirely covered with running vines and tufts of wild flowers. For long distances some of the roads are bordered with wild rose geraniums which attain a size not seen even in our conservatories at home. In whatever direction we may go we have an extended view of the ocean. Southey, the English poet, saw Cintra and said that it was "the most blessed spot in the habitable world."

Our hotel is a curiosity in its way. It is kept by an English-Portuguese family. Only one room in the house is carpeted, which is our sitting-room. We do not miss the carpets, however, for the white and well-scrubbed floors are very agreeable in this warm climate. The furniture has been in service for the greater part of the past hundred years. It was in this room that Byron wrote the lines in Childe Harold's pilgrimage :

> Lo! Cintra's glorious Eden intervenes,
> In variegated maze of mount and glen ;
> Ah, me! what hand can pencil guide or pen,
> To follow half on which the eye dilates!

Byron wrote his name with a diamond on a pane of glass in the window which commands a view to the sea. The autograph was coveted and asked for by every tourist visiting the room, until a few years ago, when some "irrepressible" traveler took the glass from the window and departed with it without even saying, "By your leave, madam."

You enter this little inn by a door-way leading three or four steps down into what appears to be the steward's room, but which is in reality the provision-room, and at the same time the guest's sitting-room and also the office of the house. The floor is frequently obstructed with chickens, ducks, and turkeys, which flutter, cackle, quack, and gobble in vain attempts to release their legs from the cords which bind them, while the mistress of the inn and the vender are earnestly bargaining. There also baskets of eggs, fruit, and cheese awaiting sale.

This is a favorite place for the guests of the house to find a comfortable chair after a fatiguing walk or donkey ride, and to await the arrival of the mail-bag with letters.

There is no end of curious details which might be mentioned respecting the inn. The cuisine is fairly good; the *chef d'œuvre* of the kitchen is a pigeon pie. A good breakfast and dinner may be had here every day.

The Portuguese mode of carrying baggage when one goes to spend a few weeks in the country is novel, and convenient to say the least. The people carry their effects in large calico bags. Two persons will each have two large bags. It is surprising to see how neatly and compactly things may be packed away in bags. This custom has its real merits. The baggage can be handled most conveniently and occupies the least possible space in a room.

A summons or call for servants, peculiar to this country and observable everywhere, is given by clapping the hands and making a hissing sound between the tongue and the teeth. This summons generally substitutes the use of bells in houses. The coachman heeds this call as well as the waiter and housemaid. The *gallegos*, who are the water-carriers and street-messengers, and who have their stands on the street-corners, look anxiously at the windows and doors, eager to hear the summons for their service. The passing fruit and fish venders recognize the well-known call; in fact, it pervades every branch of service in the country.

After five o'clock in the afternoon scores of donkeys may be seen jogging along the dusty roads carrying on green, blue, or crimson plush saddles ladies going to tea visits, or to make calls of etiquette. The donkeys are driven by boys and girls, who keep the animals in the road and from stopping to nibble grass along the roadside by a switch or twisting their tails. The ladies wear broad-brimmed sun-hats and carry bright-colored umbrellas. This mode of going about is very convenient and inexpensive. The service of a donkey and a driver may be had for a milrei (equal in value to one dollar in our money) a day, allowing the driver his usual rations of bread and wine, and the donkey a few tufts of thistles.

Cintra is the only convenient and agreeable summer resort for the Lisbonese. Usually the diplomatic corps take quintas in Cintra for six months in the year, where visiting is done with much less formality than at the capital. Donkeys are the ever-available animals on which to ride to picnics and to places in the country. Ladies are transported by them to afternoon teas, and the docile animals travel at a lively pace when urged thereto by the boys behind them with switches.

LISBON, November 29. We have seen a bull-fight, the last of the season. In the summer there is one every Sunday. A Portuguese bull-fight of to-day is not the cruel and brutalizing sport of former times, nor is it as repulsive a spectacle to look upon as a Spanish bull-fight. The ring is called a *praça*, and is like a large open circus-ring, with two tiers of boxes, one hundred in all, extending half-way around the circle. The royal box is handsomely furnished with crimson velvet and gilt decorations. Opposite this box is the grand entrance for the *cavalleiros*, or horsemen. On one side of the royal box is the entrance and exit for the bulls. There are always thirteen bulls brought out, coming in singly one after the other.

The sport begins at five o'clock in the afternoon, when the great heat of the day is over. In the morning of the day of the fight the points of the horns of the bulls are crowned with small gilded balls. The bulls are from five to seven years old. Deadly weapons are no longer permitted to be used by the *matadors*, or fighters. The weapons used are slender wooden darts, two feet long, decorated with gay-colored ribbons, and having iron bars at one end called *farpas*. The cavalleiros are gentlemen well trained in horsemanship. Sometimes the *fidalgos*, or noblemen, take part in the sport. The cavalleiros wear a costume of the last century,—broad-tailed black velvet coats, knee-breeches, with high-topped boots, cocked hats, and are mounted on splendid Arabian horses. The *bandarilheiros*, or foot-fighters, wear richly embroidered velvet jackets of various colors, knee-breeches, white stockings, black velvet slippers with broad buckles, and red silk sashes around their waists ending with gilt tassels. The director of the entertainment sits under the royal box, and gives his orders through a bugler standing by his side.

The performance begins with the entrance of a half-dozen cavalleiros splendidly mounted upon horses richly caparisoned, who make the formal obeisance to the royal box and spectators. After making some fine evolutions of old Spanish horsemanship, they retire. At a bugle-signal a bandarilheiro takes his place at one of the side doors through which the bulls enter, one at a time, he holding in each hand a dart, which he thrusts skillfully and quickly into the sides of the bull's neck as he runs into the ring. The bull, enraged by the sting of the barb, seems to know upon whom he is to avenge himself, and he plunges toward the young man in the bright jacket, but misses him, for the bandarilheiro has already jumped the partition wall and escaped, to appear at another point. The bull is goaded on by more barbs thrust by other assailants, and turns and plunges at those nearest him. After the infuriated animal has eight or ten darts dangling from his neck, the tantalizers begin to shake large red and yellow caps before him to allure him to attack them, which he does, but they by dexterous movements make their escape.

The mounted cavalleiros now come into the ring and take part in barbing the bull with a weapon four feet long. They must approach the bull near enough to place the dart in his body and yet save their horses from being attacked. Great excitement ensues, and skillful horsemanship is displayed. As the bulls become exhausted they are led out of the ring, when their wounds are dressed with salt and vinegar. The bulls are driven into town the night before the fight, and returned to the country soon after the spectacle is over. The "sport" lasts about two hours, and closes with a grand entry of all the participants, who again bow to the royal family and the audience, expressing thanks for the patronage. A bull-fight occurs every Sunday during the summer in Lisbon. But the most enlightened portions of the world regard bull-fights as relics of old-time barbarism which are out of keeping with this more refined age. Consequently there is a growing public sentiment against them, and they are becoming less popular. It is to be hoped the time is not far distant when they shall disappear entirely.

www.ingramcontent.com/pod-product-compliance
Lightning Source LLC
Chambersburg PA
CBHW020849270326
41928CB00006B/624